A NEW DAWN

A NEW DAWN

---

*Your Favorite Authors on
Stephenie Meyer's Twilight Series*

Edited by Ellen Hopkins
with Leah Wilson

"A Very Dangerous Boy" Copyright © 2008 by Susan Vaught
"The Good Girl Always Goes For the Bad Boy" Copyright © 2008 by Megan McCafferty
"Romeo, Ripley, and Bella Swan" Copyright © 2008 by Rosemary Clement-Moore
"My Boyfriend Sparkles" Copyright © 2008 by Anne Ursu
"Dancing with Wolves" Copyright © 2008 by Linda Gerber
"Tall, Dark, and . . . Thirsty?" Copyright © 2008 by Ellen Steiber
"As Time Goes By" Copyright © 2008 by K. A. Nuzum
"Destination: Forks, Washington" Copyright © 2008 by Cara Lockwood
"Dear Aunt Charlotte" Copyright © 2008 by Cassandra Clare, LLC
"A Moon . . . A Girl . . . *Romance!*"Copyright © 2008 by James A. Owen
"Edward, Heathcliff, and Our Other Secret Boyfriends" Copyright © 2008 by Robin Brande
"To Bite, or Not to Bite; That Is the Question" Copyright © 2008 by Janette Rallison
"The Great Debate" Copyright © 2008 by Rachel Caine
Additional Materials Copyright © 2008 by Ellen Hopkins

www.teenlibris.com

Developed for Borders, Inc., by BenBella Books, Inc.

Send feedback to feedback@benbellabooks.com

Printed in the United States of America
10 9 8 7 6 5 4 3 2 1

Library of Congress Cataloging-in-Publication data is available for this title.
ISBN 0-9792331-5-1

Proofreading by Erica Lovett and Yara Abuata
Cover art by Ralph Voltz
Cover design by Laura Watkins
Text design and composition by PerfecType, Nashville, TN
Printed by Victor Graphics, Inc.

CONTENTS

Introduction
To Twilight or Not to Twilight
Ellen Hopkins / vii

A Very Dangerous Boy
Susan Vaught / 1

The Good Girl Always Goes For the Bad Boy
Megan McCafferty / 13

Romeo, Ripley, and Bella Swan
Rosemary Clement-Moore / 23

My Boyfriend Sparkles
Anne Ursu / 37

Dancing with Wolves
Linda Gerber / 51

Tall, Dark, and . . . Thirsty?
Ellen Steiber / 63

As Time Goes By
K. A. Nuzum / 83

Destination: Forks, Washington
Cara Lockwood / 97

Dear Aunt Charlotte
Cassandra Clare / 109

A Moon . . . A Girl . . . *Romance!*
James A. Owen / 121

Edward, Heathcliff, and Our Other Secret Boyfriends
Robin Brande / 131

To Bite, or Not to Bite; That Is the Question
Janette Rallison / 145

The Great Debate
Rachel Caine / 157

INTRODUCTION

To Twilight or Not to Twilight

Ellen Hopkins

Tread carefully, dear readers. There's a new vampire in town, and Edward Cullen is so not your mother's vampire. Okay, he does have a few things in common with more classic bloodsuckers like Anne Rice's Lestat. He's cultured. Insanely alluring. Downright dazzlingly sexy. Drop-dead gorgeous, in fact. (Sorry, couldn't help the double entendre, and you'll find more in this book. Authors just love stuff like that.) But what makes Edward so damn addictive is not his undeadness. It's his abiding humanity.

Okay, confession. I was at first dumbfounded by the success of *Twilight* and its sequels, *Eclipse* and *New Moon.* Oh, I've always understood the lure of the vampire. For many years I was, in fact, a dedicated horror reader. Stephen King and Dean Koontz were always at the top of my reading lists, along with classic authors like Edgar Allan Poe, Bram Stoker, and Mary Shelley. When Ms. Rice came along, I devoured her books, much like her characters devoured their unsuspecting victims. If I could have faulted Rice's books, it would have been for their heavy descriptiveness, which at times overpowered the action. I preferred the pacing of King, whose storytelling fascinated me on an instinctual level that I didn't under-stand until I became a writer.

You see, as writers, we often analyze the works we loved to read. What drew us to them? Why did they work for us? What kept us turning the pages? When I went back to consider why I loved Stephen King's books, it came down to one central thing. Character. Yes, he writes high-concept plots, but they evolve from character, something I strive to do with my own books. King is the master of character. He takes ordinary people and puts them into horrific situ-ations. How they deal with them has everything to do with who they are as humans. King taps into the heart of us all—our shared humanity.

But what of this Stephenie Meyer phenomenon? She says she first pitched *Twilight* as a "suspense romance horror comedy." What, exactly, is *that*? And why would *anyone* want to read it? I didn't think I did, and I resisted for a very long time. I never read books just because everyone else is reading them. Why start with this one? A first novel, five hundred pages, inspired by a dream and written in three months? To *Twilight* or not to *Twilight*? Definitely not.

And then I started to notice an interesting fact. Her readership and mine overlap. How could that be? I don't write horror (despite the fact that I once thought I'd be the next Stephen King). Nor do I write suspense, comedy, or romance. I write edgy contemporary fic-tion. I write about drugs. Suicide. Abuse. And not the kind of abuse that results from some undead being chomping into my protago-nists. What could our books possibly have in common?

The only way to find out, of course, was to read them. And when I was asked to contribute to this anthology, it gave me the perfect excuse to do what I swore never to do—read Stephenie Meyer. I picked up *Twilight* with some trepidation. I had heard a lot about the book—both good and bad. I suppose all books have fans and what-ever the opposite of "fans" is. ("People who don't like them" is awfully unwieldy. Antonym for "fan," anyone?)

I have now read all three. Because I'm a writer, I likely read with a different eye than someone reading strictly for pleasure, and my opinion is surely colored by my own ideas about good writing and what makes a compelling read. Not to mention what makes characters interesting. Meyer, an English lit major, has said her favorite author is Jane Austen, and there is an evident Austen flavor in Meyer's writing. Her storytelling flows like a slow, steady stream, its bank lush with adverbs and adjectives. Closer to Rice than King, and definitely nothing like my own spare style, which is more a hailstorm, eroding modifiers from the page. Nope. No crossover appeal there.

Well then, how about our heroines? Meyer's Bella is flawed, and certainly, so are my female protagonists. Not a solid one in the bunch, and like Bella, all make poor decisions along their journeys. But Meyer, who has called her teen self a "regular good girl," writes her Bella as a regular good girl, too. When wronged or hurt, she tends to flee, or to withdraw into some inner sanctum where others can't touch her. I prefer to write about "irregular troubled girls." Though all of them are decent at their cores, when forced to react, they are much more likely to exact revenge than to suffer in silence. If Meyer's readers love Bella, how then can they be drawn to the young women in my books? Hmm. Quite the conundrum.

That brings us to our leading men. Meyer's readers seem to have formed two fan clubs: the Everything Edwards and the Just Jacobs. From the start, Jacob is clearly the underdog (underwolf?), but his "pack" loves him every bit as much as the other camp adores Edward. Both characters might be categorized as "beautiful bad boys with big hearts." I've definitely got a couple of those in my books. But I've also got beautiful good boys, and bad boys with miniscule hearts. So no, our heroes, if you can call them that, don't have all that much in common. What then, is the collective draw?

As I read the essays in this book, certain words and phrases kept popping up. Love. Romance. Unrequited romance. Longing. The search for belonging. Seduction. Obsession. Connection. Lack of connection. Love. Forgiveness. Passion. Fear. Fear of growing old. Love. Finally, something clicked. My books have all those elements, too. And those things go straight to the heart of us, as people. Meyer's books and my books do have something very basic in common. They speak, as Jane Austen's and Stephen King's books do, to our shared humanity.

If you ask someone what *Twilight* is about, chances are, they'll say "vampires." *New Moon?* Werewolves, of course. But if you take a good, hard look at Edward and Jacob, both are more human than monster. They long. Fear. Obsess. Seek connection. Most of all, they love, and their all-encompassing love for Bella is the kind of love every human being instinctively seeks. Stephenie Meyer's books are not about monsters. They are about people finding forever love, something that resonates not only with her readers and my readers, but all readers. For by opening those stunning book covers, we become immersed in Edward and Jacob's love for Bella and we absorb it, page by page.

And who doesn't need a little more love?

A Very Dangerous Boy

Susan Vaught

Fangirls, close your ears. You may not want to hear this. But your favorite vampire—that's right, Edward Cullen—may very well be a sociopath. You will probably have something to say about this diagnosis, but Susan Vaught makes a very good case for Edward's potential Antisocial Personality Disorder. From his impulsivity to his homicidal tendencies, the dangerous Mr. Cullen displays six of seven personality traits common to sociopaths, and it only takes three to qualify. A psychiatrist would likely have little problem affixing the APD label. Except, perhaps, if she were a fangirl?

I'm the world's best predator, aren't I? Everything about me
invites you in—my voice, my face, even my smell.

—EDWARD CULLEN, TWILIGHT

Edward Cullen.

Yes, I know, every fangirl in the universe just squealed at the mere mention of his name. And what's not to love? The young vampire in *Twilight* is handsome, romantic, and as he notes in the quote above, thoroughly enticing in every possible way.

He's also a predator, just like he says.

A dangerous, bloodthirsty predator at constant risk of murdering the girl he loves.

In fact, Edward Cullen might qualify for a diagnosis of Antisocial Personality Disorder, which is a clinical way of saying SOCIOPATH. As in dangerous, homicidal monster without a conscience.

Now, before all the screaming fangirls I previously mentioned come roaring after me with torches, pitchforks, and other implements of torture and destruction, let me make my case—or fail to make it. Give it some thought, as Bella *should* have done before giving Edward her heart.

In order to be diagnosed with Antisocial Personality Disorder (Sociopath! Sociopath!), Edward would have to meet at least three of the seven criteria, so let's start at the top: **failure to conform to social norms with respect to lawful behaviors as indicated by repeatedly performing acts that are grounds for arrest.**

What? the fangirls scream. *Edward is a moral, upstanding boy. He would never break the law.*

But he does, ladies. He does.

First and most obvious, Edward drives like a maniac. I'm not talking about just going a little too fast. I'm talking about absurd speeds, far over any posted limits. "You're going a hundred miles an hour!" Bella shouts at him as they head home from Bella's ill-fated shopping trip. "Are you trying to kill us?"

So what? That's just a traffic offense.

Yes, it is; however, in Washington state it constitutes reckless driving, a wanton disregard for the safety of persons or property, which carries a punishment of fines—not to mention up to one year of imprisonment. Driving like that is grounds for arrest, and Edward does it repeatedly. "I always drive like this," he admits to Bella. "I hate driving slow."

Moving up to more sinister and serious offenses, there's breaking and entering. Edward comes and goes from Bella and Charlie's house whenever he chooses. And stalking—or whatever you'd like to label Edward's little habit of sitting in Bella's room without her knowledge. Sitting beside her bed. Watching her without her awareness or consent. Repeatedly. "I come here almost every night," he tells her. "You're interesting when you sleep."

Next, to an even bigger crime, there's the technical point of Edward and Bella's age difference. Bella Swan is seventeen years old in every sense of the word. Edward's body stopped aging at the same point, seventeen, but in reality, Edward is around 106 years old. *One hundred and six.* Years old. That's a whopper of an age difference! And far outside the range the law allows for a defense of "mistake of age," or going out with someone who is still a minor. In point of fact and law, Edward Cullen could be arrested for dating Bella at all.

That brings us to the most serious set of offenses of all: the whole issue of "mistakes." Vampiric mistakes.

As in homicides.

Edward tells Bella that he and his fellow vampires in the Cullen family attempt not to hunt humans or feed on human blood, but he confesses, "We are still dangerous. . . . Sometimes we make mistakes."

Let's take a closer look at this concept and not rush past it or give it a glossy finish or treat it the same light, offhand, "oops" manner in which Edward presents it.

The Cullens occasionally make "mistakes."

Meaning, the Cullens occasionally commit murders.

They kill people.

They kill people.

Edward as much as tells Bella that he has killed humans before, and he knows some of his adoptive family has done the same— Emmett, for example. When Bella discovers Emmett has experienced the attraction Edward feels for Bella before, she asks, "What did Emmett do?" Then she notes, *It was the wrong question to ask*, and finally says, "I guess I know."

Not only has Edward committed homicide, he's also guilty of being an accessory-after-the-fact in Emmett's homicides, since Edward knows about them and presumably helped Emmett keep that truth hidden. How many of Edward's other family members have murdered people, and how many times has Edward helped them conceal these crimes?

And what about conspiracy to commit murder, or premeditation, or whatever you would choose to call it when Edward plans and fantasizes about attacking Bella and killing her? He owns up to his emotions about the first day he met her, reporting, "In that one hour, I thought of a hundred different ways to lure you from the room with me, to get you alone."

Let's review.

Homicide, accessory-after-the-fact to homicide(s), and conspiracy to commit homicide.

Even the most ardent Edward fan must admit—these are serious crimes.

I think it's safe to say, Edward Cullen has a long list of offenses that could get him arrested. "Failure to conform to social norms with respect to lawful behaviors." Yeah. His picture might be found right next to that little entry.

Now let's look at the second of the seven possible criteria for diagnosing Antisocial Personality Disorder: **deceitfulness, as indicated by repeated lying, use of aliases, or conning others for personal profit or pleasure**.

See? All the fangirls look triumphant. *Edward's honest, so you can't say this nastiness applies to him.*

Oh, yes, I can. In fact, that one's easy. Edward has used multiple aliases over many years. He's lied about his age. He and his family have been conning others, town after town, decade after decade. "And how long have you been seventeen?" Bella asks Edward when she's first learning about his history. "His lips twitched as he stared at the road. 'A while,' he admitted at last."

But, the fangirls argue, *that was for survival, not personal pleasure!*

I argue back that this "family" could have survived without being such prominent citizens. The handsome young doctor instead of a quiet computer repairman? The most beautiful, talented, intelligent students in high school instead of young-looking interns at some local business? A huge home and flashy, fast cars instead of functional vehicles to serve the purpose of their facades? Without all these trappings of luxury and pleasure, the Cullens and Edward could fly much lower on society's radar and get by with only a few deceptions, aliases, and con jobs. As it stands, because they choose to live beyond well, in luxurious fashion, these people must lie by action, word, or omission on an almost daily basis. That is their choice—and it is for personal profit and pleasure.

When Edward saves Bella's life, he lies about aspects of that as well. "How did you get over here so fast?" Bella inquires. "I was standing right next to you, Bella," Edward responds, even though he was clearly beside his own vehicle a moment before the accident. He then tries to deflect Bella's suspicion and curiosity at the hospital by first lying about the fact that he promised to give her an explanation, then treating her with derision when she relates her version of the accident: "'You think I lifted a van off you?' His tone questioned my sanity."

Edward, along with his entire vampiric clan, practices deceit as easily as taking a breath. Edward can and does con in the blink of an eye, almost every day of his unnatural life. Edward is honest—when it suits him, and suits his purposes, and gets him what he wants *only*. The rest of the time, sorry ladies, Edward Cullen is a professional liar.

On to the third criterion for Antisocial Personality Disorder: **impulsivity or failure to plan ahead.**

Now I know we've got you, roars the fangirl contingent. *Edward is careful. He plans everything.*

Ah, but is that true?

The day Edward meets Bella, he goes straight to Carlisle at the hospital, trades cars with his foster father, and in his own words, "By the next morning I was in Alaska." He spends a few days there, then decides that little road trip was hasty, "So I came back."

Shortly after that, again on impulse, he saves Bella's life even though it would have been better for his entire family if he had let her die. He thinks of a plausible reason for this action, but lets on to Bella, "I only thought of that excuse later. At the time, all I could think was, 'Not her.'" Edward then impulsively eavesdrops on the minds of her friends and family whenever it strikes him, intruding on the privacy of others to discover Bella's thoughts, feelings, and actions—instead of just asking her, or doing his best to find out by more ethical means.

Then, later, in one of the most pivotal moments of the story, Edward again acts impulsively by allowing Bella to attend the family baseball game. When it all turns wrong, and Edward realizes that murderous vampires are bearing down on the clearing where they're playing, he says, "I'm sorry, Bella," admitting his impulsive decisions have once more placed her in harm's way. "It was stupid, irresponsible, to expose you like this." Of course, the damage is done, and later in the tale Bella almost pays with her life.

These three factors would be enough to diagnose Edward—enough for most mental health professionals to beg Bella to be sensible about hanging around with this bad, dangerous boy. Some doctors might even encourage her parents to keep her at home under lock and key if necessary, because relationships like this lead only to bad places—like young women in the hospital, beaten, bitten, bones broken. Oh, but that can't happen to Bella, right? But . . . it does.

Wait, wait, every fangirl across the globe gasps. *That's just the minimum. Edward doesn't meet any more of the diagnostic criteria. We know he doesn't.*

Hmm. Let's see. There's **irritability and aggressiveness** (hello? Edward's psycho behavior when he first meets Bella—and the whole eating mountain lions thing). There's **reckless disregard for safety of self or others** (did I mention Edward hunts mountain lions instead of rabbits or beavers or foxes? Cheers on his brother Emmett as he hunts bears? Has Bella stay with him so he won't go murder the men who stalked her in the alley? Oh, and that driving thing again. . . . Yep, this list is endless). And sixth on the list is **consistent irresponsibility** (Edward misses a lot of days at school, doesn't he?).

Suffice it to say, we're now at six out of seven criteria met.

Sociopath could be spelled E-D-W-A-R-D C-U-L-L-E-N.

But, wait. What's this last item on the evil list of seven factors adding up to Antisocial Personality Disorder?

Lack of remorse, as indicated by being indifferent to or rationalizing having hurt, mistreated, or stolen from another.

Hey, even I have to admit that Edward Cullen is nothing if not a dark, brooding ball of remorse. Over his existence. Over his blood-lust. Over his feelings for Bella. Over *everything*. So all of you fan-girls who have armed yourselves and started hunting down my address on the Internet, you can calm down, because this is where the whole Edward-as-Sociopath argument begins to unravel.

Edward brings new meaning and intensity to the word *remorse*.

This poor century-old boy feels guilty for just about everything related to his life, family, and existence. "I don't want to be a monster," he says emphatically when Bella questions him. From the moment he meets Bella, he proves this assertion in every conceivable way. His impulsive flight out of Forks, for example, he undertakes because at his core, Edward doesn't wish to harm Bella. His return, at least in part, occurs because he can't bear the knowledge that his running away emotionally wounded his foster mother Esme. When all of this spills out of him, he tells Bella, "I couldn't live with myself if I ever hurt you. You don't know how it's tortured me."

For all of his many years (which could be considered squicky by some standards with respect to this relationship), Edward has zero emotional experience. As such, he truly is seventeen at heart, and in actions. He abashedly admits to Bella that he's never been attracted to another human being before. When he falls in love with her—and he does appear to love her—he falls so hard he can barely think clearly. "You are the most important thing to me now," he explains to her. "The most important thing to me ever." The depth and intensity of these emotions set Edward apart from most sociopaths, who only experience the most superficial of emotions.

Edward also makes repeated attempts to deny himself the very thing he wants most: Bella. At first, he tries physical distance and contrives reasons to stay away from her—yet he can't. When those strategies fail, he sets about warning her, attempting to put her off or scare her away with statements like, "That is something to be afraid of, indeed. Wanting to be with me. That's really not in your best interest." Even when Bella won't believe him or listen to him, he tries yet again, telling her, "Never forget that I am more dangerous to you than I am to anyone else." These attempts to see to the welfare of another instead of his own also separate Edward from the typical sociopath. He is delaying, even denying, his own gratification— something the garden-variety antisocial would never do. With Edward, it's *not* all about him. And his conscience is on full display in these telling moments.

When Edward's choice to be with Bella does in fact hurl her into a dangerous situation during the baseball game when other vampires arrive, Edward puts his own body between Bella and the blood-thirsty tracker intending to harm her. He's willing to sacrifice his own safety, comfort, and life to protect her—not something a sociopath would ever consider.

Edward tells Bella later that if he hadn't defended her, her life would have ended right there, in that moment. Despite this danger, he refuses to abandon the girl he loves or allow the family members she cares about to come to bad ends. He sticks right beside Bella, so close that he keeps his arm around her every second they're exposed as they make their escape from Forks. "'Fifteen minutes,' he warned under his breath." That's as much risk as he's willing to take with Bella's life. If she can't extract herself from her father in that length of time, Edward plans to snatch her from her home and force her into hiding until he can dispose of the vampiric monsters threatening her.

Edward also takes full personal responsibility for the disaster, once more showing his guilt, angst, and deep, deep feelings: "'It's my fault—I was a fool to expose you like that.' The rage in his voice was directed internally." He turns to his family for help, and he (and the rest of the Cullens) lay their immortal lives on the line to save her. They go after the hunter and his wicked female companion rather than allow the pair of hungry vampires to track Bella and kill her. Personal responsibility and making amends for poor decisions by assuming the consequences—once more, not the actions of a sociopath. Most antisocials will go to any length to blame their actions on others and never make the effort to repair damage they have done, especially damage that truly isn't their fault.

When Bella later almost dies at the hands (er, fangs) of the horrific hunter bent on taking her life, she experiences Edward's rush of feelings as a dream: "'Bella, Bella, no, oh please, no, no!' And the angel was sobbing tearless, broken sobs." A sociopath in tears over the pain of another human being? Not likely. In fact, that would just about be a miracle. Sociopaths are cold, emotionless people, not at all touched by this depth of feeling.

Even more telling about Edward's lack of sociopathic spirit— here is the perfect opportunity, the perfect excuse for him to "turn" Bella. To make her a vampire like himself and have her young and beautiful forever. Edward even has to bite her, taste her blood, to save her from the hunter's infection. Everyone would certainly understand if he can't control himself, if he gives in to temptation and drinks her to the brink of death—or if he simply refuses to take the risk and lets her go through the pain of the change into a vampire. Either way, he would have what he most desires—Bella, by his side, forever—but Edward makes a noble decision. He takes away the fire and danger in Bella's blood, eases her pain, and removes the infection instead of allowing the transition to claim her.

When Bella chastises Edward for not allowing her to become a vampire, he reminds her of the humans she would lose, like her mother and father. He tells her he won't be the one to end her life. When she tries to insist, he becomes adamant that she should live as she was meant to live and once more reveals his inner turmoil about the very fact he is even alive and in the world himself: "That's how it's supposed to happen. How it should happen. How it would have happened if I didn't exist—*and I shouldn't exist.*"

Edward then continues to put Bella first and give of himself, staying at her bedside while she recovers, day in and day out: "As long as it makes you happy, I'll be here." He even goes to excessive lengths to make sure Bella has all the experiences due her, that she doesn't sacrifice one bit of the excitement and discovery she should have as a seventeen-year-old girl. He takes her (somewhat against her will, even) to her prom. Not exactly the actions of a calculating, selfish sociopath.

Finally, when Bella once more tries to drive Edward to turn her into a vampire, he puts her off with gentleness and love. Instead of granting her impetuous wish, he declares his devotion once more with, "I will stay with you—isn't that enough?" Then he tells her that her love *is* enough for him, "Enough for forever." Hence, Edward puts Bella's needs ahead of his own in almost every way, even when she herself doesn't recognize her best interests and tempts him to do otherwise.

So how about it, fangirls? Have I saved my own life yet?

I think it's clear that on the surface, Edward represents every parent's nightmare. He's a bad boy, a very dangerous boy, and by the letter of the diagnostic law, he could be categorized as among the worst of the worst: an antisocial, a soulless sociopath, devoid of proper conscience and concern for the welfare of others. Yet when we dig below that surface, get past appearances, and really look into the heart and mind of Edward, we find a torn, tortured, and remorseful creature who wants to love, who does love, and who would give his eternal life to protect the people (and vampires) who matter to him.

"Common sense told me I should be terrified," Bella notes as she reconciles these different facets of the boy who has captured her heart. "Instead, I was relieved to finally understand. And I was filled with compassion for his suffering, even now, as he confessed his craving to take my life."

This is the crux of Edward, and perhaps the key aspect of him that moves Bella so deeply and so thoroughly. He is in many ways a monster, and he definitely has violent and unspeakable urges. He makes mistakes, and he takes reckless chances, some of which jeopardize the very people he so wishes to cherish and protect. But for all of these transgressions, Edward truly suffers, and this, more than anything, redeems him.

Edward's passion, angst, guilt—and even more importantly, his actions—lift him out of the category of *very dangerous boy* and place him firmly in a different category. You know what it is, fangirls, just like Bella, and you've known it all along. I'll admit it, too. When all things are considered and explored, this angelic vampire may be dark and treacherous, mysterious and mercurial, even arrogant and impulsive—but more than anything else, Edward Cullen is a hero.

●　●　●　●　●

Susan Vaught is the author of *Trigger*, which was called "a powerful cautionary tale" by *Publisher's Weekly* in a starred review, and *Stormwitch*, winner of the Carl Brandon Society Kindred Award. Both were named Best Books for Young Adults by the American Library

Association. Her most recent release, *Big Fat Manifesto*, is already garnering critical acclaim. She is a practicing neuropsychologist and lives with her family and dozens of pets in rural Tennessee.

The Good Girl Always Goes For the Bad Boy

Megan McCafferty

Edward Cullen may very well be the ultimate "bad boy" of every good girl's dreams. But for Bella Swan, it's not enough to dream. At a single glance of his dazzling face, she is totally smitten, and despite her screaming intuition, sets out to win him. Driven by her fear of growing old, Bella's unflinching infatuation with the definitive dangerous dude overpowers all sense of right and wrong, not to mention personal peril. To gain understanding of this seemingly inexplicable obsession, Megan McCafferty revisits her own high school years, and the bad boy poet who stole her good girl heart. And where is that guy today? The answer may surprise you.

The Twilight series has been on my should-read list for some time. I was drawn to *Eclipse* in the bookstore shortly after it came out. The striking crimson-on-black cover art—pale hands held out in offering, tempting readers with an Edenic apple—bore no resemblance to the glittery pink books surrounding it on the shelves.

Then I read the plot synopsis:

> About three things I was absolutely positive:
> First, Edward was a vampire.
> Second, there was a part of him—and I didn't know how dominant that part might be—that thirsted for my blood.
> And third, I was unconditionally and irrevocably in love with him.

Yikes. As the author of books for teens, it's my job to familiarize myself with the most popular and best-reviewed books for young adults. But I had no interest in reading a gothic love story about teenage vampires. Generally speaking, I like my teen entertainment to be based on reality. I've always been skeptical of books set in fantastic realms because the reader is at the mercy of the author's whimsy. In a world where anything can happen, ANYTHING CAN HAPPEN. Thus, the author can always cheat her way out of any tricky narrative situation by making ANYTHING HAPPEN, even if it doesn't make much sense or comes out of nowhere. (Note: This is *always* possible, of course, even in novels set in so-called real life. I'm not saying this was a *good* excuse for not reading fantasy novels, but it was *my* excuse.)

I need to see myself or others I know in the pages. Even if we don't have anything in common on the surface, I want to be able to relate, to connect with the characters on an emotional level. And not just in books, either. I mean, I never watched a single episode of *Buffy the Vampire Slayer*, but was obsessed with *Freaks and Geeks*. Frankly, I couldn't imagine having any reason to care about Bella Swan, Edward Cullen, or anyone else in Forks, a town where humans, vampires, and werewolves coexist. I hastily wrote Meyer off as a teenybopper Anne Rice—to whom she was favorably compared—and put the book back unread.

Over the next few years, Meyer's series would become an international phenomenon. *Twilight*, and its sequel *New Moon*, earned her unrivaled critical and commercial success and a rabid fan base comprised mostly of teenage girls. Though my books also sold well, even hitting the *New York Times* and other national bestsellers lists, it's safe to say that her novels outsold mine at a ratio of one bazillion to one. Though we were technically writing for the same demographic, I didn't feel competitive or jealous because I saw us as totally different types of writers. I wrote contemporary coming-of-age novels. She wrote gothic romances. *Totally different.*

But when Meyer's *Eclipse* came out on the same day as my fourth novel, my professional curiosity was, um, piqued—to put it mildly. I had scheduled a series of drop-ins at bookstores, during which I would meet and greet with booksellers and sign stock. Over the course of a single day, while I stood at various customer relations desks autographing stacks of my new novel, I watched no fewer than two dozen teenage girls run into the store, squeal with crazed delight at the sight of *Eclipse*, and run to the cash register as fast as their flip-flops could carry them. A few paused long enough to notice me scribbling my name on the inside cover of my own novel. More than one of those girls gasped in recognition, then shared an approximation of the following comment: "Marcus Flutie and Edward Cullen are neck-and-neck for the hottest fictional character ever. Ha! Ha! No pun intended! Ha ha!" (Okay, the lame bloodsucker joke is mine. I couldn't resist.) While it was flattering for my Marcus Flutie to be so favorably compared to the iconic Edward Cullen, I was a bit surprised to hear this. What could my flesh-and-blood bad boy share in common with a bloodthirsty vampire? And would this answer bring me any closer to understanding why Meyer's books inspired such passion among the young women I saw in the bookstores, and millions more like them?

It turns out that the answers to these questions were: Quite a bit. And: Yes.

I read *Twilight*, *New Moon*, and *Eclipse* in the span of three weeks and made what was for me—as a newbie to the high school vampire scene—a startling discovery: Meyer hasn't rejected high school realism, she has repurposed it. And in doing so, she has revitalized the tried-and-true trope of a million teen romance novels (including my own), in which the ordinary heroine gets seduced by the irresistible rebel. Oh, it would have been enough for Bella Swan to fall for Edward Cullen if he had simply been a gorgeous, class-ditching, brooding baaaaaaad boy with a troubled family history, like Marcus Flutie and so many other anti-heroes in teen fiction. But Meyer ups the (wooden? Sorry . . . I couldn't help myself again . . .) stakes by making Edward a gorgeous, class-ditching, brooding, baaaaaaad boy with a troubled family history who JUST SO HAPPENS TO BE A VAMPIRE. A vampire who has to fight every instinct not to give in to the lure of Bella's delicious scent, tear into her flesh, and feast on her blood.

Of course, Bella doesn't know this right away. She just knows that there's this brilliant, beauteous outsider who seems to hate her on sight. Paired up as lab partners in biology class, Edward sits as far away from Bella as possible. "He was glaring down at me again, his black eyes full of revulsion," Bella says. "As I flinched away from him, shrinking against my chair, the phrase, *if looks could kill* suddenly ran through my mind." Oh, how portentous those words turn out to be. . . .

If Edward had continued to show contempt for Bella, it's unlikely that she would have gotten caught up in his undead world. It's only so long that the beautiful bad boy, even one blessed with a "dazzling face," "gloriously intense eyes," and "flawless lips," can mistreat you before you write him off as a total asshole. But true to the bad boy's mercurial nature, Edward can be as warm as he is cold (metaphorically speaking, anyway). When he finally deigns to speak to Bella (only after going on a hunt, quenching his thirst for blood, and dulling, though not totally quelling, his urge to fill up on *her*) he forgoes the small talk and goes straight for her heart (also only metaphorically). He asks probing, provocative questions, making it clear that he wants to know her like no one else does. "I couldn't fathom his interest," Bella says, "but he continued to stare at me with penetrating eyes, as if my dull life story was somehow vitally important." What high school girl doesn't want to fascinate the most fascinating boy in school? Bella is compelled to tell all, though she's still not sure why: "I was in disbelief that I'd just explained my dreary life to this bizarre, beautiful boy who may or not despise me."

Bella will later learn that Edward's first feeble attempts to distance himself are for her own protection. Every time Edward forbids Bella from getting too close, arguing that they can't ever be friends, they can't ever do the unthinkable and *fall in love* because he is bad, oh-so-irredeemably bad, his warnings have the opposite effect. Bella inches closer, she can't stay away. She falls hard, hopelessly and irretrievably. "No matter how real the danger might be," thinks Bella, "*It doesn't matter*."

Meyer has brilliantly played into that ineluctable law of high school attraction. All good girls get obsessed with at least one bad boy, and the danger of *what will happen next* is a huge part—if not all—of the appeal. The risk for Bella is of a supernatural nature: Edward's love could quite literally kill her. The peril a real-life good girl puts herself in when she chooses to pursue such a relationship is less severe, though no less terrifying: She can ruin her reputation. Her standing among her family and friends. And her sense of self-control.

I should know. I was the very best of the good girls. And my fevered-and-frigid, off-and-on and always off-limits friendship with the very worst of the bad boys at my high school was just about the only thing that relieved the monotony of my junior and senior years.

> How much have you changed little girl? All I know is
> that you've earned the title old friend. Have the vam-

pires gotten you too? Is that why you seem so alien lately? Why you seem so angry? Why you threaten me with your claws and fangs? They must have gotten to you when I wasn't around. . . .

I'm sure I don't even need to tell you that the above passage was not written by Stephenie Meyer. No, I'm quoting from a note furtively passed to me seventeen years ago by said bad boy in the hallway in between classes. His bad boy credentials? Numerous suspensions for cutting class, fighting, public drunkenness and countless other infractions, a failed urine test or two, a possible stint in rehab, and of course, a reputation for (ahem) fuck-and-running. To add to his mythic persona, it was rumored that this baddie had an IQ that tested off the charts in elementary school and just couldn't be bothered with the baa-baa-sheep mentality of the American educational system. He was often seen hunched over his notebook writing cryptic, hallucinogenic poetry, or sketching pictures of mythological beasts with talons, fangs, and outrageous phalluses. My good girl qualifications? I was voted Most Likely to Succeed and Teacher's Pet in my senior class superlatives. That should be enough proof for you.

Why am I telling you this? Because Meyer's trilogy, more than anything else I've ever read, brought me back to those days of being irrationally and irresistibly drawn to this inconceivable boy. The more the chattering masses at Central Regional High School voiced their collective disapproval, the more I wanted to prove them wrong. What could possibly be more compelling than off-limits romance? After the first hush-hush phone calls and tightly folded and re-folded notes, I, like Bella, knew it would be "smart to avoid him as much as possible . . . to go back to ignoring him as much as I was able. . . . To tell me to leave me alone." And also like Bella, I dismissed that option immediately because the thought of enduring the dreariness of my high school days without the promise of our conversations and letters left me "gripped in sudden agony of despair."

As I regressed deeper into the heart and mindset of my seventeen-year-old self, it became increasingly clear why this series is so enormously popular: Meyer has perfectly captured the intensity of one's first forbidden infatuation. Bella and Edward's risky relationship serves as a stand-in for readers' own unspoken desires, their own longing to be reckless in romance.

And, um, it's all pretty erotic, too. The sexual subtext in *Twilight* is particularly delicious. "It's not only your company I crave," Edward tells Bella. "Never forget *that*. Never forget that I am more dangerous to you than I am to anyone else." But how can Bella resist? Especially when Edward can use his powers to break the rules and sneak into her bedroom every night (swoon!), undetected by her disapproving father. How can she stop her heart from pounding when Edward is so obviously agonizing over the damage he knows he can do to her? When her every throbbing heartbeat pounds the very blood Edward thirsts for more than anything else? Bella is so overcome by the power of his touch that she literally passes out after their first kiss. Is it any wonder then that by the third book in the trilogy Bella not only yearns for the supernatural transcendence of "the change" but also the very human pleasures of the flesh, becoming the sexual aggressor who wants to see, to *feel* what would happen if they, you know, did *it*?

It's at this point—when Bella wants Edward's body in exchange for her soul—that their good girl/bad boy roles reverse themselves. Like many girls who overestimate the transformative significance of losing one's virginity, Bella longs to be bitten so she can become "strong and fast and, most of all, beautiful. Someone who could stand next to Edward and feel like she belonged there." Edward understands that the venomous transformation is far more complicated and painful than Bella's fantasies and wants to spare her the agony of eternal damnation. So it is Edward who is always trying to stop the relationship from going too far, and Bella who is hell-bent (literally . . . ?) on crossing the boundaries between the human and vampire worlds, between life and death, and what comes after. Edward repeatedly tries to put Bella off, first by using "mind over matter" to control his baser impulses, as so many horny teenage boys have done throughout history. When that fails, he leaves town with no explanation in *New Moon*, hoping that his hasty exit will break Bella's heart but hopefully inspire her to give up her vampiric designs and choose life instead. This enforced forgetting backfires when Bella repeatedly puts herself in harm's way—motorcycle riding and cliff diving and pursuing a friendship (and more) with Jacob Black, a werewolf and natural enemy of vampires—just to hear the sound of his voice trying to stop her, even when those warnings are only a figment of her imagination. Long after they are reunited, Edward continually begs Bella to reconsider her plan to be bitten, going so far as to encourage her to attend Dartmouth College and "enjoy a normal, happy human life."

Over the course of three books, Bella is increasingly irrational and impulsive while Edward grows more responsible and—daresay—conventional. Meyer brings this point home in *New Moon* and *Eclipse* when Edward realizes that Bella's "impatient human hormones are [his] most powerful ally." He finally agrees to have sex with Bella *and* turn her into a vampire, but only on the most virtuous of conditions: she must marry him first. In one of the most amusing passages in the whole series, Bella says, "You make me feel like a villain in a melodrama—twirling my mustache while I try to steal some girl's virtue." To which Edward replies, "I had no right to want you—but I reached out and took you anyway. And now look what has become of you. Trying to seduce a vampire." It's another interesting twist on the predator/prey relationship. Bella is horrified by the idea of getting married at eighteen years old, but begrudgingly agrees to it when she realizes it's the only way she will get what she wants: Edward in body and soul.

There's a sense of urgency throughout *Twilight*, *New Moon*, and *Eclipse*, driven by Bella's dread of getting older. Every tick of the clock separates her that much more from the unchanging teenage vampire with whom she has so foolishly fallen in love. However, given Edward's shift from rebellion to responsibility, I can't help but wonder if Bella is unconsciously trying to stop *him* from changing any more than he already has. But that's just because I know firsthand what effect seventeen years of living has had on my own bad boy, that mysterious force of nature who wrote me lines like,

> You run at me and kill me. Trying to seduce me with your venom so you may become one of your following cadavers, but my biological makeup is much different and the poison has no effect. You realize I'm immune and choose to ignore me, since you won't help and can't hurt me. . . .

I know he has become a churchgoer, a regular productive member of society, a loving husband, and devoted father of three kids. Writing him a perfunctory e-mail to ask permission to write this essay was not fraught with anxiety, exhilaration, or anything at all resembling the fiery fascination he ignited back in high school. And like the thoughtful adult he has grown up to be, this former bad boy wrote me back within the hour, mocked his morbid poetry, and suggested a pseudonym (Shrek) inspired by one of his kid's favorite cartoon characters. He had become, in a word, *ordinary*.

I can only assume that Meyer—who, like me, is twice Bella's age—also knows the fate of such foolhardy youthful infatuations. Bella wants her love for Edward to be preserved for all eternity just as it is: extraordinary. As a vampire, Edward has an advantage over other fictional rebels like Marcus Flutie, and the real life high school hell-raisers who grow up, grow old. Edward Cullen has the potential to remain forever passionate, forever young. And for that alone, I don't blame Bella or any of Meyer's fans for falling in love with him.

• • • • •

Megan McCafferty is the *New York Times* bestselling author of *Sloppy Firsts*, *Second Helpings*, *Charmed Thirds*, and *Fourth Comings*. She lives in New Jersey with her husband and son, and is at work on the fifth and final book in the Jessica Darling series. To read her (retro)blog, visit www.meganmccafferty.com.

Romeo, Ripley, and Bella Swan

Fate and the Classic Hero in the Twilight Universe

Rosemary Clement-Moore

Okay, trivia fans. What does the movie *Aliens* have in common with the classic Greek tragedy *Oedipus*? Time's up! How about this one: What does Shakespeare's *Romeo and Juliet* share with the Jim Carrey movie *Liar, Liar*? Beep! How do all of the above relate to the *Twilight* series? Rosemary Clement-Moore, a theater major, explains that Meyer's books invoke in readers the two elements central to all classic tragedies (not to mention *Aliens* and *Liar, Liar*)—sympathy and fear for heroine Bella Swan. Why do we pity her? And what are we afraid of for her? Clement-Moore offers her insights.

This is hard for a literature geek—not to mention a theater major—to admit, but here it goes: *Romeo and Juliet* nearly killed my GPA freshman year. I just didn't get it. I feel vaguely heretical admitting that. The play contains some of the most beautiful (and quotable) language ever written, but it took me a long time to understand why it's a classic.

What does this have to do with Stephenie Meyer's lushly engrossing, gothic tale of Bella Swan and her vampire lover? When I first read *Twilight*, I remember thinking that it was a little like *Romeo and Juliet*, except one of them is already dead. Then I opened *New Moon*, and the first thing I saw was a quote from Shakespeare. Within the first chapter, Bella and Edward are discussing the similarities (sort of) between their relationship and Shakespeare's famous tragedy. It's nice to know, as a reader, that you're not just imagining things.

Meyer uses these parallels to good advantage. Most of the time, when you read a novel as romantic as *Twilight* and its sequels, you expect everything to work out in the end. One of the strengths of Bella's story, at least for me, is that it never loses the sense of jeopardy. Meyer doesn't shy away from hurting her main characters. The happy ending does not feel like a forgone conclusion. The allusions to *Romeo and Juliet* are a reminder that love does *not* conquer all. In fact, sometimes it can really screw things up.

But the series has more in common with classic tragedies than the danger of ending up with a stage full of dead bodies before the curtain comes down. Bella's story—her romance with Edward, her position between the werewolves and the vampires, her complicated relationship with Jacob—harkens back to the classic hero, fate, and the idea of a destiny determined by a trait so intrinsic to the hero that it cannot be changed, no matter what the consequences.

In other words, it's not any plot similarity that makes Bella's story feel like a classic tragedy, but rather that the elements that go into it are the same elements that have, for thousands of years, resonated with audiences. To examine this, we have to go way back, past Shakespeare, to about 300 B.C.E., when a Greek philosopher named

Aristotle came up with theories about literature that still affect how we think about art, even in the twenty-first century. (I *did* warn you I was a theater geek. But stick with me, folks.)

In Aristotle's day, if you wanted a good story, you couldn't just run down to the Borders at the corner of Athens and Sparta and buy a novel. People went to the theater. You might think a play in Ancient Greece wouldn't have much in common with the high-tech spectacles on Broadway now, but really only the technology has changed. People went to the theater then for the same reason we go the movies or read a book now: to laugh or cry, to be horrified or amazed, to be entertained or informed.

There were comedies and epics, and there were tragedies. The tragedies are the ones we usually have to study in high school: *Oedipus* and *Antigone* and all their multitudinous family problems. The curriculum guides don't drag these out just to depress senior English students (as convincing as that theory might seem). The lasting impact of the literature has to do with the intent of the tragedy versus the comedy.

Classic comedies illuminate the human condition by drawing broadly exaggerated examples of the worst traits of mankind. I am going to loose my Thespian Society secret decoder ring for making this comparison, but—think of Jim Carrey in *Liar, Liar*. He plays a habitual liar who is "cursed" so that he can only speak the truth. The character starts at one extreme—Carrey plays a slick and insincere lawyer who lies to his own son—and ends up at the other—he is compelled to blurt out the truth about even trivial things, like who farted in the elevator.

The ridiculous problems that result from Carrey's exaggerated honesty point out how much we, as a culture, lie—white lies, lies by omission. Classic comedies are intended to comment on human society as a whole. Tragedies, however, should connect with the spectator on a more personal level.

The goal of the classic tragedy was to evoke emotions of pity and fear in the audience, to make them feel as if they were living the story themselves. By experiencing these emotions through the action on stage (or on the page, once mass-market publishing came along), we learn about our place in the universe.

We feel pity for the classic hero, because even though his own actions lead to his fate, he generally doesn't deserve what he gets (hence the word "tragic"). The hero learns through his suffering, and because we sympathize with him, we learn, too. For example, Gloucester in *King Lear* loses his eyes because he did not see his sons' treachery until too late. It makes us realize the value of being able to see, both literally, and figuratively, what is going on around us.

Since I've already confessed that I have some *history* with *Romeo and Juliet*, I'm going to use another great classic as an example. In this case, a movie: James Cameron's *Aliens*.

(You don't think Aristotle would approve? I said I was a literature geek, not a literature snob.)

In *Aliens*, our hero is Ripley, last surviving crewmember of the *Nostromo*, a spaceship where everyone gets massacred by an eight-foot-tall, armor-plated, acid-dripping alien monster. She escapes and puts herself in suspended animation for the long trip back to Earth, and when she gets there, fifty-seven years have passed. Her daughter has grown up and died. The world has changed and she's alone in it. She loses her pilot's license, gets a lousy job, and is so plagued by horrible nightmares that when some yutz wants her to return to the planet where the thing came from, that's actually her best option.

Unlike Jim Carrey's character in *Liar Liar*, Ripley didn't do anything to deserve this. When she and a team of space marines reach the alien planet, she is forced, again, to face the monsters that killed her old crew and left her alone in the universe. She befriends Newt, a stranded little girl (because every alien-infested planet needs a precocious orphan girl), which leads her into even worse trouble, because when the acid hits the fan, she cannot leave her comrades, especially Newt, to die horrible deaths at the hands—claws—of the aliens.

So let's talk about Bella Swan. On the surface, she seems pretty much on top of things. She makes decent grades, takes care of her dad Charlie, cooks dinner every night. Though she made the decision to move to Forks, she seems to view it as the lesser of two miseries: living in a strange, sunless place with Charlie, or living with her mother, Renée, who just remarried, and preventing her from following her new baseball player husband on the road. The latter isn't a viable alternative for Bella; there is only one choice that she can make, and it carries her to her destiny.

In Forks she meets Edward, and things spiral out of her control. He calls her a "magnet for trouble" and that certainly seems to be true. Within the first fourth of *Twilight*, she's nearly squashed by Taylor's van, faints in class, and runs into a gang of thugs on a trip to Port Angeles. Not to mention how she's always tripping and falling. (Could her clumsiness be a metaphor for what she really is: not just a klutz, but a classic hero, blown around by the whim of fate? Or is her clumsiness a reversal of the Greek dramatic concept of *deus ex machina*? Instead of the gods appearing at the end of the play to fix the character's problems, are the Fates constantly "tripping" Bella up to cause problems, and keep her on her destined path?)

Later in the book, things get truly dire when Bella attracts the attention of the killer vampire James. Not just any carnivorous vamp, but one with an obsession for hunting. He's like the Terminator: once he's got her scent, he will never stop. Not only is her life in danger, but Renée's and Charlie's as well. It looks, for a while, like we could be headed for that tragic stage full of dead bodies.

And what has she done to deserve this? Nothing but fall in love with Edward. You could argue that wasn't wise—Jacob fans certainly would—but you can't say that she did anything wrong.

And so we sympathize with Bella Swan. But that sympathy is only half of the equation. Aristotle says that, to really move us—to change us through our experience of the story—drama must evoke both pity and fear. If you only have pity, you feel sorry for the character, maybe you have a good cry, but then you close the book and go on with your life unchanged. To stick with you, the story has to evoke fear as well.

"Fear" in this case isn't the same as shock or horror. (Not that Greek drama lacked gory or shocking plots. I mentioned Oedipus' family problems, right?) The fear or dread in classic tragedy is based on our emotional connection with the hero.

We have to sympathize with the hero in order to put ourselves in her place and feel her fear as if it is our own. In *Aliens*, we're afraid for Ripley because we don't want to see her splattered all over the screen by a chest-busting ET. But we also fear that she won't succeed in rescuing Newt from the Alien Queen. Because we sympathize with her—that she's already lost two "families" in her first crew and her biological daughter—we can put ourselves in her place and understand the stakes for her.

I admit it's unlikely that any of us will be trapped on an alien-infested planet, fighting for our lives against a hive of extraterrestrial killing machines. But Shakespeare wrote about the problems of nobles, princes, and supernatural creatures, and for the Ancient Greeks, the heroes of their dramas were kings and demigods—in both cases, the characters are as different from their intended audiences as Ripley and her space marine comrades are from us.

This disparity between hero and audience is important to the classic tragedy. It forces us to realize that if kings and queens and space marines are at the mercy of the Fates, then so are we.

So coming back to twenty-first-century Earth: What makes Bella bigger than life? Her distinctive scent, maybe, which links her inexorably with Edward. Or her immunity to his mind-reading, which seems at first to be something unique to their relationship, but we see later extends to other, similar vampire "magic," including Jane's illusionary torture in Italy.

If this were an adventure novel, these things might make her into a superhero. But the emphasis is put less on what her mysterious immunity means for her and more on what it means for her relationship with Edward. In the same way that Romeo and Juliet's love for each other defines them, what really makes Bella special is her ability to inspire love and loyalty in two extraordinary boys—Edward and Jacob.

Beauty has nothing to do with it. She describes herself as average-looking (though some of the events in the books make me wonder if she isn't judging herself against the—as-yet—unattainable perfection of the Cullen family). Yet she has *two* super-gorgeous, super-powerful, supernatural guys in love with her.

Of course, this causes a world of trouble for her and brings danger to her family and loved ones. As it is for kings, princes, and alien-killing spaceship pilots, the thing that makes Bella special and different is the same thing that drives her destiny. If not for that, we might feel only jealousy. Instead, we feel sympathy for her; we connect with her as a tragic hero.

So if she's got our sympathy, then what do we fear for Bella? The threat of antagonist vampires is constant through the books, first James, then the Volturi, and finally Victoria and her army of newborns. But Bella doesn't seem to really fear death, so why should we?

It comes around, again, to love. Some readers are afraid that she'll be parted from Edward. Some are afraid she'll never see Jacob again. But all of us—whether we realize it or not—are afraid of what the loss of love will do to her. The thing we fear for her is Ripley's fate: that those she loves will leave her, and she will be alone with a ragged hole in her heart.

In *New Moon*, Edward doesn't just leave her, he takes all the evidence he's even been there—the CD of his composition for her, his picture in her album. He erases himself not just from her present and future, but from her past. In response, she becomes like the walking dead—which is ironic, when Edward fights so hard against turning her into a vampire.

"Time passes," Bella tells us from the depths of her grief, "even when it seems impossible. Even when each tick of the second hand aches like the pulse of blood behind a bruise."

Through our sympathy for Bella, we experience that heartbreak along with her. And we fear, because if this can happen to Bella Swan, who is so special that she has earned the love of two amazing boys, how can *we* be safe if we give our heart that deeply? Can we even avoid it? Or are we, like Romeo and Juliet, or Bella and Edward, at the mercy of fate?

That's what the Greeks dramatists believed, and it's the last knot in the cord that runs from the playwrights in Aristotle's time, to William Shakespeare, to the romantic story of a girl who loves a vampire.

English teachers like to talk about the "fatal" or "tragic" flaw in classic heroes: Macbeth's ambition, Othello's jealousy, Hamlet's indecision (or excess deliberation, depending on what side of that argument you're on), or Antigone's loyalty to her brother. These are the "flaws" that lead these heroes, and very often those around them, to their fate. That fate may not be death, but if you're familiar with any of those plays, you know the body count is usually pretty high in the last act.

But Antigone's loyalty isn't really a "flaw." Neither is Ripley's need to rescue those trapped by the aliens, or Bella's love for Edward. Yet those are the things that lead them to their destiny.

Ripley, from the moment she woke up from hypersleep, was only going to end up one place: face to face with the alien. Likewise, *Romeo and Juliet* could only end in tears, whether or not death went along with it.

Obviously, I'm not going to be able to avoid Romeo and Juliet entirely, especially when, in *New Moon*, the parallels are so obvious—something that Meyer weaves, with self-awareness, into the plot of the book. She opens, remember, by quoting the play itself:

> These violent delights have violent ends
>> And in their triumph die, like fire and powder,
>> Which, as they kiss, consume. (*Romeo and Juliet*,
> Act II, Scene vi)

Shakespeare's metaphor is not entirely about the destructive power of love. Like heat and gunpowder, from the moment Bella and Edward meet, there is an inevitability to what happens. Their passion is strong, violent in intensity, even though it starts with what appears to be passionate *dislike* on Edward's part.

He sits through their first class together as stiffly as if he's ready for battle, his fist clenched so tight that the tendons stand out in his forearm. He stares at her, "his black eyes full of revulsion." Bella flinches away from him, thinking, "if looks could kill."

Not exactly the flirtatious, love at first sight, which happens between Romeo and Juliet.

Or *is* it?

We could say that it's love at first whiff. Bella smells irresistible to Edward, though not in a romantic way. The battle he is fighting is against himself, but also against fate. He skips class, tries to change his schedule, and does everything he can to avoid her and the hunger she evokes.

But despite his efforts, he can't stay away from her. He eavesdrops on those around her, and protects her from danger even when it puts him in peril of revealing his supernatural nature. It would be a lot easier for him if he could have let Tyler's van flatten her, but he can't, and not just because he has too much humanity. He is connected to her, compelled to stay near her against his better judgment.

Part of this may be her compelling scent, or the curiosity of her immunity to his mind-reading ability. But none of this explains

Bella's fascination with Edward. While some girls like guys who seem unattainable, that doesn't seem to fit with Bella's personality.

She feels a deep and indelible bond to him, one that develops more quickly than the intensity of their meetings—and his frequent rescues of her—can explain. It's true passion, the "violent delights" that Shakespeare compares to the combustion of gunpowder. Not only physical passion (though obviously that's a factor), but an emotional attachment that defies reason.

In *Twilight*, Edward describes his feelings: "For almost ninety years I've walked among my kind, and yours . . . all the time thinking I was complete in myself, not realizing what I was seeking. And not finding anything, because you weren't alive yet." Then just a few paragraphs later, he explains the difficulty involved in Bella choosing to be with him: "You only have to risk your life every second you spend with me . . . You only have to turn your back on nature, on humanity . . . what's that worth?"

Despite Edward's worries, Bella never doubts that she loves him, and wants to be with him, even though they face a much more serious problem than feuding families. Predator versus prey trumps Montague versus Capulet by anyone's measure.

Everything that happens springs from this connection between Bella and Edward. She encounters James and Victoria because Edward has introduced her to the Cullens. When Edward rescues Bella and kills James, it sets Victoria on a path of vengeance, and her continued presence in the region leads more of the Quileutes to become werewolves—including Jacob. (Members of the tribe only make the change to werewolf when there is a threat nearby. Jacob blames the change in himself and his friends on the Cullens at first, but the increase in boys getting furry is more likely due to Laurent hunting in the region while he scouts on behalf of Victoria.)

Their relationship, and the loyalty that Bella inspires, also brings the Quileutes and the Cullens into an uneasy partnership to fight the invading band of newborn vampires. The ensuing battle, injury, and death are all tragic elements, and though the major players emerge without permanent physical damage, we can't dismiss Jacob's broken heart, or Bella's anguish at his departure from her life.

"A pair of star-cross'd lovers" (*Romeo and Juliet*, Prologue), Bella and Edward are fated to fall in love. They cannot do differently, because that is how the winds of fate blow their ship of destiny. Instead of calling her a "magnet for danger" we could call Bella the same thing that Romeo calls himself: "Oh, I am Fortune's fool" (*Romeo and Juliet*, Act III, scene ii).

Fate is inescapable in classic tragedy. In Homer's saga, *The Iliad*, a seer predicts that baby Paris will grow up and cause the fall of Troy, so baby Paris is left on a hillside to die. But the kid is favored by the gods: He's nursed by a bear and found by a shepherd, who brings him back to Troy, where Paris grows up to start the Trojan War by running off with the wife of the King of Sparta.

Homer has the gods to interfere in the heroes' lives and keep them on their destined path. Bella has vampires and werewolves. Unlike the Ancient Greeks, most of us in the twenty-first century don't think much about fate. Bella's story works so well as a fantasy because once you accept the idea of supernatural monsters, a pre-destined love at first sight seems like no big deal. Werewolves "imprint" (sometimes very inconveniently, as we see in *Eclipse*) and it seems with the other Cullens (Alice waiting for Jasper, Rosalie saving Emmett after the bear attack) that when they meet their true love, they know it.

Edward has been around for ninety years and knows when he meets Bella that she is special to him. The Volturi even have a word for someone whose blood calls to him the way hers does—*la tua cantante*, a singer. But Edward is not a killer, and when he resists the call of Bella's blood the two become something new and unique.

If they are destined to fall in love, despite the problems it presents, at least they can learn from how badly things turned out for Shakespeare's couple. Couldn't Bella and Edward change their path?

They both contemplate this in *New Moon*. Bella considers the alternative to Juliet's choice to fake her own death: believing Romeo had left her, what would happen if Juliet married Paris? Could she find some happiness?

But even though Bella decides to make a different choice than Juliet and stay with "Paris" in the person of Jacob, who loves her, it doesn't change her fate. Almost the instant she makes that decision, Alice arrives back in Forks. Bella chooses the vampire—Edward's "sister"—over Jacob without hesitation, and she is once again on the path that fate has outlined for her.

Edward, on the other hand, makes Romeo's choice, and it's that which brings Bella back to him. They're reunited, like Romeo and Juliet are reunited in the tomb. But for Bella and Edward, their story isn't quite over yet. Will they be permanently united in living death, as Bella plans? Or is their fate to love and lose each other, which would be, as Bella has already experienced in *New Moon*, another kind of living death?

We don't know yet where the path of destiny will lead Bella, Edward, and their families. Normally, the modern audience is conditioned to expect a happy ending, but by tapping into our classic literary roots, Stephenie Meyer has given us the feeling that there is no guarantee of that in the Twilight saga. We have a story full of sympathetic characters and a central hero who is special and different, and we feel her pain, and fear for the seeming inevitability of her heartbreak.

As things stand now, there doesn't seem to be a way to avoid the loss of someone Bella loves. Jacob has already distanced himself. If Edward turns her into a vampire, Bella will have to say goodbye to her parents. If he does not, she will grow old and he will not, and they will eventually be separated by death. Neither can we forget the ramifications of him turning her: Edward will see himself as the destroyer of her soul. The bite will also cause the end of the treaty between the Cullens and the Quileutes, meaning that Bella must lose one supernatural family or another however she chooses.

Our sympathy for Bella is tied up with the inevitability of what we fear for her: that she will lose something important, some piece of her heart, whether it's Edward, her parents, her vampire family, or her second love, Jacob.

But it isn't all doom and gloom. The Classical Greek concept of fate is that your end destiny is written, but how you reach it, and how you face it when you get there, is not (even Alice's visions are subject to change). What keeps us compulsively reading is our fear that things cannot possibly turn out okay, and our hope that somehow Bella will still be all right—that whatever she is left with, it will be the thing that helps her bear the loss of the rest. That she will not be alone.

And in the nature of all classic tragedy, from Antigone to Juliet to Ripley, what we are really hoping is the same for ourselves. That whether our fate is to love or to lose, we will be okay.

* * * * *

Rosemary Clement-Moore's love/hate relationship with *Romeo and Juliet* was furthered by too many summers doing outdoor Shakespeare festivals in the Texas heat. The only tragedy she really enjoyed working on was *Macbeth*, because it involved handsome, sweaty guys in kilts.

She now puts her drama queen tendencies to use writing books. Her Maggie Quinn: Girl vs. Evil novels are a series of supernatural mysteries about a psychic girl detective (who just happens to be a literature geek and movie buff).

My Boyfriend Sparkles

Or, First Love at Twilight

Anne Ursu

Falling in love with a vampire is a lot like skating on spring ice. Fun. Forbidden. Thrilling in its unique way. And that pulse-pounding, goosebump-raising excitement has everything to do with omnipresent danger. Stay close to shore, you'll probably be okay. But you definitely don't want to get swallowed down into the cold, murky depths, and there's just no way to tell how far you can go before that happens. Some might say falling in love with anyone is like attempting thin ice. But add ever-present peril, hunger for immortality, and all-encompassing desire, and the picture grows just a little darker. Anne Ursu poses the question: Should love mean risking the shadowy depths?

Each night I ask the stars above
Why must I be a teenager in love?

—Dion and the Belmonts

Bella Swan thinks of her relationship with the vampire Edward Cullen in great sweeping terms—Romeo and Juliet, Catherine and Heathcliff. And their story certainly has echoes of those iconic lovers; they are star-crossed, ardent, destined for each other, eternal, doomed. But as extraordinary as their relationship is, it is also quite ordinary, and familiar. The overwhelming intensity of their romance makes sense because Bella and Edward are teenagers, and never is the rhetoric of star-crossed love and eternity so plausible as at that time in life. While Edward isn't exactly human, their relationship is very much so, and its course closely follows familiar tropes of teen love, for better or for worse. Bella Swan's relationship with Edward Cullen is immortal, dangerous, forbidden, impassioned, all-consuming—in short, exactly like any first love.

With Bella, Edward says he is breaking all the rules, but in reality, their relationship follows every one of them.

I Was Nothing Before I Met Him

As typical a first relationship as this one is, Stephenie Meyer portrays Bella as a very untypical teenager. Bella is somehow apart from the experience of adolescence—she can't seem to relate to her peers and to her parents she is more caretaker than daughter. And once in Forks, she's a complete alien. When she meets Edward, Bella is totally unmoored and miserable, living in a town she hates with a father she barely knows, having to adjust to a new high school where she can't seem to operate on the same wavelength as the other students, and where gym is a daily requirement. She is the consummate new girl, lonely and awkward, without even a real home to go to at the end of the day. She begins the story utterly lost and ungrounded, in desperate need of something to center her.

Bella's just different. She likes classical music, doesn't have a cell phone, isn't into dances or shopping, drives a beat-up old truck, and when she finally finds a real friend for herself it's a fifteen-year-old werewolf from the Indian reservation. But all of this difference really just makes Bella an entirely normal teenager—that sense of isolation, of deviation, is an unfortunate rite of adolescence. Meyer has taken this familiar experience and heightened it by throwing Bella into a new, uncomfortable environment, but few teenagers really feel they fit in. And nothing helps alleviate that like falling in love.

As Soon As I Saw Him, He Became My Whole World

Immediately, Edward provides the axis for Bella's emotional orbit. Even though his first response to her is angry and hateful, she can't stop thinking about him, and even when he's absent from school she lives her life in reaction to him—she's depressed, she can't sleep. Her moods become entirely dependant on him and his reaction to her. Edward is a predator, and his allure and hypnotic charm are part of his particular natural predatory attributes, but anyone who has been in love knows what Bella's going through. The experience has actually been formally pathologized by psychiatrists. Swiss researchers at the Psychiatric University Basel actually studied teenagers in love and found that they experienced intense moodiness, sleeplessness, and mania-like behavior. Another group of psychologists found that the brain of a teenager in love is similar to someone on cocaine—in other words, love is like an addiction. As if anybody needed researchers to tell them any of this.

For Edward, too, the immediate attraction is overwhelming—Bella is exactly his type, or at least his blood type. Where Bella is immediately consumed by Edward, Edward immediately wants to consume Bella. For him, Bella is not cocaine, but rather heroin. Their relationship isn't the traditional love at first sight—Bella is too awed and Edward just really wants to eat her, but nonetheless they are entrapped the moment they see each other just as if they were normal teenagers struck by Cupid's arrow.

He's Not Like the Other Boys

Bella immediately attracts the attention of some of the boys in school, but she has no interest in them—she doesn't even seem to live on the same planet. But, like Bella, Edward is apart from his classmates; the Cullens seem to operate entirely separate from everyone else. Bella immediately identifies them as fellow misfits, and that's certainly part of Edward's appeal.

But Edward isn't just apart from his peers—he is above them. Bella is like the high schooler dating a college guy because high school boys are just *so* immature. He's not just different, he's better, and this makes him both more attractive and more inaccessible to Bella.

From almost the beginning, Bella senses that something is different about Edward. There's his beauty, certainly—which she perceptively describes as "inhuman." And there's something otherworldly about him—his cold hands, the electricity of his touch, the mutability of his eyes, the fact that he always seems to have eavesdropped on conversations he could not have heard. But even on a human level, he's different than the other boys in school. Mike, Eric, and Tyler are all nice enough, and all very eager for her attention, but like a girl who believes anyone who is interested in her can't possibly be worthy, Bella isn't interested in them. Their very friendliness is what makes them unattractive to her. Edward, though, is cool (quite literally) and reserved. And when he does start acting friendly toward her, he doesn't make the well-meaning but inane small talk of the other boys; he probes into her reasons for being in Forks. Everything about him is different: his antiquated name, his nice clothes, his shiny car, and his taste in music—you get the distinct impression none of the other boys could identify "Clair de Lune," and Bella never gives them the chance. When the school dance approaches, the other boys all ask her out in turn, while Edward lingers in the background, cool and wry in direct contrast to their overeager sincerity. Tyler, Mike, and Eric want Bella to appear on their arms in this most traditional of high school rites; Edward wants to accompany her on her escape from it. The boys are common; Edward is sophisticated. They like her for being the new girl; Edward likes her for who she is. They are overwhelmed by bio labs and English papers; Edward has done them all before and knows all the answers. They follow Bella around like puppies; Edward remains alluring and remote. While the motivations of the other boys are far too easy to understand, Edward remains mysterious.

He is not like the other boys. "I'm trying to figure out what you are," she tells him in *Twilight*. A superhero is her first thought, something between Peter Parker and Bruce Wayne. "Edward Cullen was not—human," she thinks. "He was something more." She does not say something *else*, something *different*, but something *more*—better, more evolved. Not a boy, but something special.

When He Touches Me, It's Electric

When Edward and Bella brush hands in biology class for the first time, she feels "an electric current" pass between them. That feeling is so common as to be cliché—except traditionally there isn't a vampire involved in the experience. Meyer is unclear as to whether Bella's being figurative or literal, but either way the reader knows exactly what Bella means.

Researchers have actually documented the physical effects of love—it increases your adrenaline and institutes a reaction similar to the "fight or flight" response to fear. (In Bella's case, "fight or flight" is probably a healthy reaction to Edward.) In this relationship, Edward's effect on Bella physically is so powerful it often seems she won't survive their interactions. In his presence, Bella frequently forgets to breathe, or her heart stops beating, or she gets dizzy. Once she actually faints. When she sits next to Edward during a movie in biology class as their relationship is developing, his proximity nearly

drives her insane. Again, he is a predator and supposed to be alluring, but he seems to react the same way to being close to Bella, and
not out of the desire to have her for a snack. From almost the beginning, their attraction—and sexual tension—is physically palpable,
and while Meyer leaves open the possibility that there's something
mystical going on, nothing about it is necessarily out of the ordinary.

I'm Not Good Enough for Him

Bella places Edward on such a high pedestal at first that she can't
even imagine he would feel the same way. Everything about him
seems in opposition to her—his elegance and grace are in sharp contrast to her pathological klutziness. When she realizes she's excited
to go to school in order to see him, she knows she's being stupid: "I
was well aware that my league and his league were spheres that did
not touch." Her certainty affects her perceptions of all their interactions, and so when Edward mysteriously warns her that it would be
better if they weren't friends, she assumes it's because he doesn't
want to lead her on. Even when he begins to show interest, she
assumes she likes him much more than he could possibly like her.
The reason, to her, is patent:

> "Well, look at me. . . . I'm absolutely ordinary—well,
> except for bad things like all the near-death experi-
> ences and being so clumsy that I'm almost disabled.
> And look at you." I waved my hand toward him and
> all his bewildering perfection.

Even when they go on their first date—the hike in the woods—
she can't help but see herself only in opposition to him. As they are
about to embark on their hike, he (rather unnecessarily) unbuttons
his shirt to reveal his "perfect musculature" and Bella thinks, "He
was too perfect, I realized with a piercing stab of despair. There was
no way this godlike creature could be meant for me."

It's an unfortunately familiar power dynamic in relationships—the girl so convinced of her own inadequacy in the face of an out-of-reach boy that all she can see reflected in the boy's eyes is her own deficiency. In this case, though, Edward really is in a different sphere: His beauty is inhuman, and he is godlike. But, as so many girls experience, because she has put him on a pedestal Bella can't see the truth—that her crush is no god.

I Love Him So Much It's Scary

Edward spends a lot of energy giving Bella mysterious warnings that she should stay away from him, warnings that only serve to pique her interest. Her first thought, that he is a superhero, depends on her belief in his essential goodness. And even when he tells her he is dangerous, she responds, "But not bad. . . . No, I don't believe that you're bad."

Edward is a god, Edward is wonderful, Edward is better than the other boys, better than other humans. Bella has elevated him so much, and is so in love that she can't see anything else. Even when confronted with the truth, she is so convinced of his essential good-ness she cannot engage with it. When Jacob Black tells her the leg-end of the cold ones, she goes deep into the woods at night to think—maybe not the brightest act for someone who suspects vam-pires are real—and considers her options. If he is a vampire, she could avoid him as he keeps telling her to do, but:

> I was already in too deep. Now that I knew, *if* I knew I could do nothing about my frightening secret. Because when I thought of him, of his voice, his hyp-notic eyes, the magnetic force of his personality, I wanted nothing more than to be with him right now.

Bella has made her decision—in fact she believes there's no deci-sion to make. She is in love with him, and nothing else matters. Like a "bad boy" boyfriend with a checkered past—or a major self-esteem problem—Edward tries valiantly to convince Bella he's no good for her, but she sees nothing but the superhero she loves.

Both of them act like insecure teenagers with each other, believing if the other *really* knew them, he/she would leave them. When Edward finds out Bella has been talking to Jacob, he is visibly tense, clearly sure that when she discovers who he really is, she'll run from him. But Bella stops him short when she says, "I decided it didn't matter." Edward is incredulous:

> "It didn't *matter*?" . . .
>
> "No," I said softly. "It doesn't matter to me what you are."
>
> A hard, mocking edge entered his voice. "You don't care if I'm a monster? If I'm not human?"
>
> "No."

The depth of Bella's feelings serves to terrify him—not because he doesn't share them, but because it means there's no going back. Ironically, for Edward, the prospect of the relationship is far more terrifying than it is for Bella. Like the stereotypical teen boy, he is "afraid to commit"—but for most boys it's not because they're worried they might eat their girlfriends. For Bella, it's all irrelevant. She has no choice, because she would quite literally rather die than be without him.

Bella is not the first girlfriend to overlook her boyfriend's flaws, but at times like this, Bella and Edward's relationship has darker overtones. Edward is a monster, but Bella can't see it, and she makes excuses to herself and to Jacob. Bella needs to be with him, even if the consequence is her own death.

He's Not Sure He Can Control Himself with Me

Bella fancies their relationship as epic, ideal, but the very fact that Edward is a vampire who hungers for her blood necessitates a dynamic where she is always floating between girlfriend and potential victim. The day before their planned walk in the woods, Bella senses that the date will be pivotal in their relationship—but the real question seems to be whether or not Edward can control his lust for her blood. Still, Edward seems determined to test himself—perhaps idiotically so, given his idea for a great first date is to hike five miles into the woods to a secluded clearing no one else knows about.

In any other story, what follows would be a sex scene. When Edward reveals what really happens to vampires in the sunshine, Bella begins to stroke him in an extremely intimate scene, like lovers bare with each other for the first time, dazzled by the beauty and closeness of the other. But the intimacy cannot last, and Edward has to dash away so he doesn't kill her. As he has to remind her, "It's not only your company I crave! Never forget that. Never forget I am more dangerous to you than I am to anyone else." It creates an odd sexual metaphor, with Bella as the virgin girl whose boyfriend isn't sure he's going to be able to help himself.

The message for teen girls is so often that boys are predators, that they only want one thing, that they can't help themselves, that you have to be constantly on your guard lest they take advantage of you. Perversely, then, it becomes the girls' responsibility to protect themselves; since boys are sex-crazed id-machines, they don't have to take responsibility for their actions.

Edward is anything but sex-crazed; still, Bella takes it as her responsibility to keep him from being tempted—not for her sake, but for his. Even before their date she distracts herself from her nerves by concentrating on "making things safer for him" in case he should lose control. When she responds too lustily to him, she beats herself up, portraying herself, strangely, as the perverse one, unable to keep herself from responding to him. The relationship, then, must remain not physical, and like a couple committed to abstinence this informs all of their physical contact.

Edward certainly considers it his responsibility to keep himself in control (for once, here, it is the guy who is interested in protecting his virtue). And for Bella, this internalization of society's messages may actually be a weird form of denial—by worrying about protecting Edward, she doesn't have to think of the danger to herself. By casting herself as the responsible one, she can believe she is in control. While the consequences are literally life and death for her, the impulse is entirely ordinary; the human brain eagerly reshapes reality in service of love, and Bella's is no exception.

I'll Love Him Forever

Despite everything, Edward and Bella are addicted to each other, with all the heady irresistible passion of love. Like so many real couples, they become completely wrapped up in each other, to the exclusion of everyone and everything else. "I love you," Bella tells him. "You are my life now," he responds. Even Edward, almost a century old, has never felt like this before—"For almost ninety years," he tells her, "I've walked among my kind and yours . . . all the time thinking I was complete in myself, not realizing what I was seeking. And not finding anything, because you weren't alive yet."

It's a lot for a seventeen-year-old, and like any parents afraid of their daughter's first relationship, Bella's parents fret. Her father warns, "He's too old for you," without knowing the half of it. He worries she's spending too much time with Edward, ignoring her other friends; he grounds her until she spends time with other people, and even tries to have a sex talk. Her mother is concerned that Bella's too young to be in love, and Bella lies, "It's just a crush."

Her parents are worried that the relationship is too intense, and for good reason: Bella soon begins to think in terms of forever. "Forever" is a common trope in first relationships (the writer and former British prime minister Benjamin Disraeli wrote, "The magic of first love is our belief that it will ever end"). Bella decides she has to stay with Edward, at whatever cost.

After Graduation, I'll Die

But the clock is ticking. Like a high schooler growing more wary as the shadow of graduation encroaches, Bella feels the inexorable movement of time. Their relationship has to have an end point, and Bella sees it coming; she is going to grow older, and Edward is not. (Curiously, with Jacob Black she plays a game where they assign each other varying ages based on personal qualities—with Edward, age is fixed and doom-laden, whereas with Jacob it's mutable and fun.) What she was trying to ignore becomes a reality, and every moment they move closer to the inevitable.

The anxiety is potent and real. The problem with high school romances is what happens after graduation—is the relationship truly forever? What happens when people age and change? And are you in any position to make decisions that determine the rest of your life? Edward's plan is the common solution—"We'll go to college together!" And, "We'll get married!" But Bella has other ideas. She wants to become a vampire. Being with Edward forever is worth any sacrifice, including that of her family and her soul. She lamely brushes off the impact on her parents: "I was hurting them more by staying human," she tells herself. "I was a danger magnet" (*Eclipse*).

Like a mother concerned her daughter is wasting her youth on one person, Edward keeps trying to convince Bella not to waste her humanity, not to sacrifice her soul. But she can see nothing but being with Edward, cannot really understand the consequences of her choice, and instead of paying attention to Edward, who really loves her, ultimately puts the question of her fate to Edward's family—a bunch of vampires. And when she sees how newborn vampires behave—like animals, thinking of nothing but the hunt—she worries not that she'll hurt someone, but that she won't have the same desires for him physically.

> "I won't be the same! I don't know who I'll be then."
> "You'll still be Bella," he promised.
> I frowned. "If I'm so far gone that I'd want to kill Charlie—that I'd drink Jacob's blood or Angela's if I got a chance—how can that be true?"

Just as she dismisses the consequences to her mother and father, Bella treats the idea of lusting after her friends' and family's blood rather offhandedly. Far worse, it seems, would be not lusting after Edward. The question of her soul she dismisses as well. "If you stay," she tells Edward, "I don't need heaven."

When Bella's parents worry about the intensity of their relationship, this is what they are afraid of. Not that she'll become a vampire but that, because of her youth, she'll make a foolish choice that she'll regret. Her parents got married too young and divorced right after Bella was born, and they don't want her to make the same mistake. And Bella's commitment is going to be far more permanent than marriage.

New research into brain development posits that the area of the mind responsible for judgment doesn't develop until we're in our twenties. This has lead to theories of a "teenage brain"—pleasure-seeking, intense, addictive, reckless—and has given some adults ammunition for arguments that teenagers shouldn't make life-long decisions (like marriage or, say, becoming a vampire). Whether or not that's true, Bella clearly isn't thinking with the judgment-area of the brain. Bella is being rash, dangerous, foolish—but it's to be expected; she's young and in love.

My Boyfriend Sparkles

With Edward everything is *more*—he is more beautiful, more out of reach, more alluring. Touch is more charged, sex is more dangerous, and forever is an eternal commitment. But the story is still a familiar one: Bella is apart from her peers, more adult than child, not expecting to find love anywhere but desperately needing something to give her an anchor. Edward is every girl's fantasy—gorgeous, chivalrous, distant, mature, a well-manicured outsider, dangerous, yet at the same time guaranteed not to put on any sexual pressure. Both think of themselves as unworthy of the other; both cannot function without the other. And when they are together, nothing else matters—not parents or friends or encroaching vampires. They are each other's whole world. And when they lose each other, they are utterly lost. Bella becomes lost to blackness. Edward seeks death. Their emotions, their rhetoric, is extreme, but not unrealistic. Everything is heightened in their relationship, not because Edward is a vampire but because being in love, especially as a teenager, makes things heightened—intense, dangerous, romantic, epic, exhilarating, and with eternal consequences.

Of course, Edward is a vampire. These books are fantasy. But the best fantasy tells us something about reality. The author Lloyd Alexander said, "Fantasy is a good way to show the world as it is. Fantasy can show us the truth about human relationships and moral dilemmas because it works on our emotions on a deeper, symbolic level than realistic fiction." The Twilight series is certainly successful in showing us this over-examined experience—first love—in a new way, letting us examine it with fresh eyes. We feel for Bella because we understand feeling unworthy of someone. We understand someone so intensely that nothing else matters; we understand desperately wanting to have forever and the terrible anxiety that we won't get it. The reasons might be different here, but the feelings are the same, and the experience utterly human.

But the story is not a perfect vehicle, and there are aspects to Bella and Edward's relationship that, when translated into the real world, become disturbing and dangerous. Edward is a god—truly inhumanly beautiful, predatorily alluring, and better at everything than she is—and a monster, and both aspects set up troubling dynamics in the relationship. Every physical interaction is informed by the possibility that he might lose control, and the real-life echoes of these interactions are closer to violence than love. Bella's all-consuming ardor for Edward can be disturbing, too—fantasy or not, it's unsettling for a teenage girl to lose herself so thoroughly in her boyfriend that she can only think of protecting him in case he should kill her.

As well, Bella and Edward are not equals, and Edward's need to protect her means he is often controlling her, ordering her around, carrying her against her will. It's so expected for him to control her that it's treated as perfectly acceptable when he has Alice kidnap her so she won't spend time with Jacob. His superior abilities mean she is always the one in the role of victim, needing to be saved, her only power in battles her ability to draw her own blood.

Then there is the question of forever—an even more impossible problem in a vampire love story than a high school romance. In order for them to be together forever, Bella has to make a terrible choice—to become a monster, someone who could very well kill others—and in order to make it more palatable, Meyer needs to eclipse the true nature of that choice.

This story is fantasy, no more realistic than vampires—but the very nature of the fantasy romanticizes the relationship and obscures elements that in reality would be disturbing. Bella and Edward's love is impassioned, beautiful, eternal—but not perfect. As Bella could tell you, high school love is hard enough; high school vampire love really bites.

* * * * *

Anne Ursu is the author of *The Shadow Thieves* and *The Siren Song*, fantasies for young readers, as well as two novels for adults. She currently lives in Ohio with her husband, baby boy, and an increasing numbers of cats. She used to have nightmares about vampires, but is pretty much over it now.

Dancing with Wolves

The Spiritual Journey of Quileute Lycanthropes

Linda Gerber

> Many people have a fascination with wolves, and so we find them in myths and legends throughout history. From the ancient Mongols to the modern Inuit, storytellers have linked wolves and humans. But is the connection merely a sort of primal respect for an animal that shares our rung on the food chain ladder? Or do we, perhaps, see ourselves in them—or them in ourselves? Could this be where the numerous legends of lycanthropes (werewolves) began? Linda Gerber shares tales of wolves and werewolves, including the lupine legends of the very real Quileute tribe.

The wolf's eyes were dark, nearly black. It gazed at me for a fraction of a second, the deep eyes seeming too intelligent for a wild animal.

As it stared at me, I suddenly thought of Jacob. . . .

—NEW MOON

I might as well confess up front—I'm one of *those* people: a diehard Jacob fan. Not that I don't love Edward, mind you, but there's something accessible and familiar about Jacob that Edward, in all his stone-cold beauty, can't touch.

Jacob doesn't have Edward's years of experience or polish. He's naïve, he's rash, and he's delightfully primal. And when we learn the boy is part wolf, he's irresistible.

It's only natural, that attraction; we humans have a certain fascination with *canis lupus* that can't be denied. Look at all the wolves that pop up in our myths and legends throughout the millennia. We can't get enough of them.

As Daniel Wood puts it in his book *Wolves,* these animals are "mirrors, reflecting the proximity of the primitive in human nature." No wonder we're so fascinated with wolves. We see ourselves in them. Wolves, after all, share many of our same characteristics. They're social, like us. They care for each other and hang out together in communities. They are involved parents, as we would like to believe we are. Wolves share our territory. They are exceptional hunters and are one of the only species besides man who can communicate and work together as a pack. Their howling, as Wood says, is "poetic, even in its bloodthirsty nature." That music appeals to us. We can relate to wolves on our most primitive level.

This could be why wolves have played such a significant role in history, culture, and spiritual teachings all over the world. Civilizations as diverse as the ancient Mongols (who claim the wolf as their ancestor)[1] to the Romans (whose wolf-god Wepwawet was said to have accompanied the pharaoh on his hunts) believed that wolves held special power.

Wolves even presided over the heavens. Norse myths tell how Sköll chased the sun across the sky and Hati chased the moon. In

---

[1] Mongol mythology holds that they descended from a gray wolf and a white doe.

China, the star Sirius—called the Celestial Wolf—stood guard over a great palace in the constellation of Ursa Major.[2]

Wolves in mythology were ultra cool—powerful, intelligent, amazing. Is it any wonder stories emerged to illustrate the intimate relationship between wolf and man? It's that mirror thing, remember? We want to see ourselves reflected in that coolness.

The stories suggest varying degrees of kinship with wolves. A wolf served as protector and guide to the mother of the Chipewan and the Inuit.[3] She-wolves nursed human children in myth and modern literature.[4] Bella Coola[5] and Turkish[6] stories tell of coupling between a human and a wolf.

The coolest stories of all, though, let the human actually *become* a wolf. Legends of lycanthropes are known in almost every part of the world, and not just in fireside tales, either. Werewolf references found their way into such respected works as Plato's *The Republic*

---

[2] The red star, Sirius, also known as the Wolf Star, is the brightest star in the northern sky. In China it is called *T'ien-lang*, or Celestial Wolf. Its charge is to guard the celestial palace of Shang-ti, the home of the heroic dead. Native American legends also hold that Sirius is the home of the Ancients. The Milky Way is the wolf's trail—the route into heaven.

[3] A Canadian Dene Tribe myth tells of a wolf that led a mother and her two young children to safety from their enemies. Her two sons grew up to father the Inuit (Eskimo) and Chipewan people respectively.

[4] Roman mythology tells of Romulus and Remus, the founders of Rome, being nursed by a she-wolf. Recently, archeologists discovered a shrine in a cave where they believe ancient Romans worshiped Lupa, the wolf that suckled them. It is called, logically, the Lupercal shrine. In more modern literature, Rudyard Kipling had the main character of *The Jungle Book*, the boy Mowgli, nursed and raised with wolf cubs.

[5] Bella Coola legends tell of a man who married a wolf in human form. They lived together with their child in the wolf village and eventually the man became a wolf.

[6] Turkish legend tells of a small Mongolian village in northern China attacked by enemy soldiers. All were killed but one baby. A she-wolf named Asena nursed the baby, after which she gave birth to half-wolf, half-human cubs—the ancestors of the Turkish people.

and Pliny's *Natural History*. The Greek historian Herodotus even wrote of a tribe of people—the Neuri—who lived in what is now modern-day Poland and changed into wolves once each year.

Jacob's people also had such stories of man taking on the characteristics of a wolf, and a wolf becoming a man. Stephenie Meyer may have made up the Quileute history of the spirit army and their shape-changing ways in the Twilight books,[7] but the actual myths surrounding Native Americans' close relationship with the wolves are legion.

The very origin of the world is tied to the wolf in many tribes, even though they might disagree on detail. Blackfoot legends tell of Old Man, who created the world from a ball of mud and set a wolf free to run across the surface, shaping valleys and plains. According to Cree legend, Wisagatcak the Trickster enlisted the help of Wolf to help create the world from a ball of moss. The Akira of the Great Plains tell a similar story featuring Wolf-man and Lucky-man as creators of the earth. The poor wolf had to go it alone in Piute legend, floating along the primeval waters as he did his creating.

Some Native American myths tell of the creation of the wolves themselves. In the American Southwest, for example, Hitchi legends tell how a shaman made wolves by striking two pinecones together.

The divine nature of the origin of wolves lends extra significance to the legends of the Quileute, who are said to be their descendants. Legend has it that in the wanderings of Kwa'iti—a supernatural

---

[7] From Stephenie Meyer's Web site: "The Quileute (*Quill*-yoot) legends Jacob tells Bella in chapter six of *Twilight* are all genuine Quileute stories that I learned when I was researching the tribe (which is a real tribe with a truly fascinating and mystical history). All actual Quileute legends, except for the vampire myth about the 'cold ones.' I latched onto the wolf story (the actual Quileute legend claims that the tribe descended from wolves transformed by a sorcerer) because it fit with my sketchy knowledge of vampires and werewolves always being at each others' throats (ha ha, pun intended)."

transformer, or a "being put on earth to change things and make them better"—he came upon the area known as La Push and transformed two wolves into men—the first members of the Quileute tribe.

Regardless of the particulars, one thing the native stories agreed upon was the sacred nature of the wolf. If wolves mirrored man in general, they mirrored Native American people even more specifically. Their tribe is the pack. Their chief is the alpha. Cooperation and dedication to the group are essential to their survival.

Jacob and his werewolf brothers take it a step further; their spiritual selves are tied to the wolf as well. In the Quileute and other Olympic Peninsula tribes, wolves provide spiritual strength to its warriors and may serve as spirit guides to tribal members. Vision quest stories and rituals such as the crawling-wolf dance prominently feature wolves. In the case of the Quileute boys, they *are* wolves. Accepting, learning, and becoming their true selves represents a spiritual growth of epic proportions.

On a journey toward self-discovery or spiritual awareness, the average person hits his or her first major identity crisis or bump in the road about the same time as puberty. The response is typically rebellion, experimentation, resistance to authority—an increased yearning to "find oneself." From there, said average individual normally gets to enjoy the self he or she finds for a decade or two before hitting another speed bump. Poor Jacob and brothers are still figuring out life as adolescent boys—a tough enough job in its own right—when they are hit with the mother of all identity crisis: coming to terms with the fact that they are also wolves.

Take Jacob's transformation into a wolf pack-member, for example. The Jacob of *Twilight* is young, raw, and inexperienced. He knows of his people's legends, but in his mind they are an abstract. They are part of a mythical history, but have little to do with him. In fact, his tone as he relates the legends to Bella at First Beach is almost dismissive.

> "There are lots of legends, some of them dating back
> to the Flood—supposedly, the ancient Quileutes tied
> their canoes to the tops of the tallest trees on the
> mountain to survive, like Noah and the ark . . .
> Another legend claims that we descended from
> wolves—and that the wolves are our brothers still.
> It's against tribal law to kill them."

Imagine his surprise in *New Moon* when he finds out the legends
are real! His reaction is classic: denial, anger, avoidance—as if he is
in mourning. In fact, Jake *is* mourning. The life he knew, the person
he was, is gone forever. Dead.

His despair is evident when Bella reaches out to him.

> "Jacob, please . . . Won't you tell me what happened?
> Maybe I can help."
> "No one can help me now." The words were a
> low moan; his voice broke.

Jake avoids Bella. He fights against what is happening to him,
looking at it not as a birthright, but as a cross he is being made to bear.

To be fair, it's understandable that he would feel blindsided by
his first transformation. He had been taught the Quileute legends,
but he didn't realize how literally they pertained to *him*. Jacob was an
innocent, and when he "turns," he is torn away from his old life and
thrown into a position where he *has* to learn the secrets of his society.

Coincidentally, actual wolf ritual initiations throughout the
Olympic tribes mirror Jake's experience as an unsuspecting innocent. One ritual in particular, *Tluukwaana*, reenacts the story of
Yanamhum, an ancient young hero who was stolen from his home.
Wolves taught Yanamhum the secrets of their society and then sent
him back to his people to pass on this new knowledge. In the *Tluukwaana* ritual, members of the wolf society (in Jake's case, those members would be Sam Ulley, Jared, Paul, Embry Call, Seth Clearwater,

etc.) capture initiates and take them to a secluded Wolf House. There, the initiates would be instructed for several days about their heritage, values, and responsibilities as members (brothers) of the secret Wolf Society before being returned to the village.

In the Quileute tribe itself, a similar tale of gaining power and instruction from wolves is enacted in a masked ritual called *Tlokwali*, or "wolf ritual." The ritual is thought to have originated with the Kwakiutl and passed to the Quileute through the Makah, and the Kwakiutl name for the ceremony, *klukwalle*, meant "to find treasure," meaning to receive gifts from a spirit.

But gifts, spiritual or otherwise, are not always happily accepted. Jacob, and indeed all the wolf brothers (except Quil, of course),[8] are not exactly thrilled in the beginning to find that they are "monsters."

> "This shouldn't be happening. Why? Why?" His fist slammed against the tree. It wasn't a big tree, slender and only a few feet taller than Jacob. But it still surprised me when the trunk gave way and snapped loudly under his blows.

As with any gift of knowledge or power, with Jacob's inception into the pack comes added responsibility—that of not only watching over his people, but of adhering to the strict rules of the pack, a restriction that would be hard for any teenage boy . . . especially one with a crush on a vampire-loving girl. But adhere he does, because to not do so would be to endanger not only himself, but his wolf brothers as well.

Now this is the law of the jungle,
As old and as true as the sky,

---

[8] Gotta love Quil Ateara for embracing the coolness of becoming a werewolf. How classic that he imprinted on a two-year-old!

And the wolf that shall keep it may prosper,
But the wolf that shall break it must die.
As the creeper that girdles the tree trunk,
The law runneth forward and back;
For the strength of the pack is the wolf,
And the strength of the wolf is the pack.
—Rudyard Kipling

At least the Quileute boys don't have to go through the same kind of testing to prove their wolf-worthiness as some Pacific Northwest tribes. Some of these trials were merely uncomfortable, such eating cold food and taking cold baths—the type of conditions they would face as warriors anyway. But other trials, such as those found in the Makah rituals, expected initiates to gash their arms and legs in a grid pattern to prove their strength and courage. The scars from these deep wounds would be recognizable to other members in the order.

The Quileute pack, of course, doesn't need any kind of scarring to be recognizable. They grow. Their muscles harden and define. They mature. Even someone outside the tribe can recognize the difference. Bella does in *New Moon*: "What was up with these Quileute boys? Were they feeding them experimental growth hormones?"

With all the reverence for wolves in the Native American culture, legends still exist that paint the shape-shifters in a vengeful light. One such legend is of the *chindi*, a creature that acts as a sort of avenging angel. It can inhabit any animal, but will usually choose something fierce, like a wolf or a coyote.

According to Navajo tradition, an animal harboring a *chindi* would walk upright, like a human. Sound familiar? One significant difference between a *chindi* and a werewolf, however, is that you can only stop a *chindi* by drawing a medicine circle around yourself and singing or chanting a prayer for protection. Silver bullets are useless. In fact, if you kill one animal host the *chindi* will simply enter another animal, and then another and another until it serves its vengeful purpose.

The Quileute werewolves have the potential to be vengeful, like the *chindi*. Many of them weren't happy to have had the werewolf life thrust upon them. They phased because of their lineage—and because the time had come that they needed to protect their lands and their people from the "cold ones." As Jacob says in *New Moon*, "[W]e only protect people from one thing—our enemy. It's the reason we exist—because they do." Jake and his friends could easily have chosen to take their unhappiness out on the local vampire family, but they know they have to exercise control and honor the treaty with (and ultimately work together with) the Cullens.

In fact, self-control[9] is one of the first things the Quileute boys have to master. If they don't, they could inflict harm on the innocent. Sam learns that the hard way with Emily. He, "lost control of his temper for just one second . . . and she was standing too close. And now there's nothing he can ever do to put it right again." Jacob comes very close to learning the same tough lesson: " . . . Billy said I looked weird. That was all, but I just snapped. And then I—I exploded. I almost ripped his face off—my own father!"

Lakota Sioux Chief Yellow Lark once prayed, "I seek strength, not to be greater than my brother, but to fight my greatest enemy— myself." A lot of religions teach a similar philosophy—that a big part of spiritual growth is to put off the "natural man," to overcome impulses and to act with morals and conscience. Jake seems to feel himself as an enemy when he says, "The hardest part is feeling . . . out of control . . . Feeling like I can't be sure of myself—like maybe

---

[9] Note that we're talking self-control as they phase. As Stephenie Meyer said in a Q&A with the Twilight Lexicon, "The danger of being around werewolves (in my mythology) does not stem from the idea that they would attack someone because they can't control themselves in their wolf forms. It comes from the fact that they can't control that transformation. In the beginning, they pretty much explode into their wolf forms whenever they lose their tempers."

you shouldn't be around me, like maybe nobody should. Like I'm a monster who might hurt somebody." He understands the importance of maintaining control over his natural man—or natural wolf, as the case might be. Jacob and his friends do not choose to let the monsters—or enemies—within govern their actions.

An old Cherokee legend[10] tells of a grandfather who was explaining to his grandson the battle that goes on inside of people.

> "My son, the battle is between two wolves inside us all. One is Evil. It is anger, envy, jealousy, sorrow, regret, greed, arrogance, self-pity, guilt, resentment, inferiority, lies, false pride, superiority, and ego.
>
> "The other is Good. It is joy, peace, love, hope, serenity, humility, kindness, benevolence, empathy, generosity, truth, compassion and faith."
>
> The grandson thought about this for a minute and then asked his grandfather, "Which wolf wins?"
>
> The old Cherokee simply replied, "The one you feed."

A tremendous part of the spiritual journey is learning which wolf to feed. Often, the natural instinct is to give in to the Evil wolf. When times are hard, it may be easier to wallow in anger, envy, resentment, and sorrow than to be humble, find faith, exercise compassion, or feel empathy . . . especially for your enemy.

Yet that is exactly what Jacob and his friends have to do in order to work together with the Cullens in *Eclipse*. And perhaps harder still, it is what Jacob has to do to protect Bella. Understanding the love that she feels for Edward, and knowing that Bella would choose to become Jake's natural enemy—a vampire—he nonetheless works

---

[10] There are many versions of this story in circulation, some claiming origin and naming various tribes, but I'm recounting it as told to me by Rattlesnake Annie. Annie herself is part Cherokee, so I'm going with her version!

together with Edward to keep her safe. (Granted, he does give in to
to the impulse to antagonize Edward as much as he can while doing
so. . . .)

In the end, Jacob has to let go of who he thought he was so that
he can become who he is meant to be. He becomes the embodiment
of the powerful spiritual symbol that is the wolf. Wolves are considered teachers and pathfinders, and through his spiritual growth,
Jacob achieves that distinction.

> His voice (was) slow and different. Aged. I realized
> that he sounded suddenly older than me—like a par-
> ent or a teacher. "What I am was born in me. It's part
> of who I am, who my family is, who we all are as a
> tribe—it's the reason we are still here."

It's no accident then that Jacob chooses the wolf part of himself
when he needs to escape upon receiving Bella and Edward's wedding
invitation. As a wolf, he can forget. He can choose serenity.

> If the silence in my head lasted, I would never go
> back. I wouldn't be the first one to choose this form
> over the other . . . I pushed my legs faster, letting
> Jacob Black disappear behind me.

My first conclusion while writing this essay was that in Jake's
decision to leave his human self behind, his spiritual journey was
complete.[11] But then I started wondering about the Native American

---

[11] Spiritual shape-shifting in Native American culture is akin to receiving their
totem animal in a vision quest. As Brad Steiger explains in *The Werewolf Book*,
"They experience the transformation in order to glory in the sense of strength
and personal freedom of the animal as it runs through the forest trails and the
mountain paths . . . spiritual shape-shifters desire to incorporate the power and
insights of the pure wolf spirit into their own psyches."

custom of vision quests.[12] What might Jacob learn on his own in the wilderness?

Perhaps his journey has just begun.

Wolf I am
In darkness
in light
wherever I search
wherever I run
wherever I stand
everything will be good
because Maheo protects us.
Ea ea ea ho.
—Tsistsistas (Cheyenne) Wolf Song

● ● ● ● ●

Linda Gerber is the author of two S.A.S.S. novels, *Now and Zen* and *The Finnish Line*, and the upcoming YA mysteries, *Death by Bikini*, *Death by Latte*, and *Death by Denim*. She lives and writes in Dublin, Ohio.

---

[12] Vision quests involve a period of fasting, meditation, and physical challenge in the wilderness, away from the tribe. The goal is to connect with one's guardian spirit and to receive a vision meant to guide one's path through life.

Tall, Dark, and ... Thirsty?

Ellen Steiber

So you think you're a vampire expert? Maybe so, but consider this. Long before the word "vampire" first appeared in 1734, rumors of undead creatures who fed on the living circulated in almost every culture. As Ellen Steiber tells us, these legends evolved from ancient beliefs in demons, witches, and ghosts. Distilled to their very core, they were rooted in the human fear of relinquishing the dead to whatever afterlife did or did not exist. Throughout the centuries, tales of vampires became more sophisticated and perhaps, at least in Steiber's view, less about our fear of dying and more about our paranoia of growing old.

As Stephenie Meyer tells us, stories of vampires have been around for centuries and have appeared in almost every culture. Although it's hard to make definitive statements about vampires, their history, or their lore, I think it's safe to say that vampires were not originally conceived of as romantic heroes. They were threatening and tremendously creepy, monsters who caused fear and revulsion. They were a far cry from Meyer's Cullen family, a clan of the undead who are so dazzlingly beautiful and good that when Bella seeks to give up her own mortality to join them, this reader's first reaction was: *You go, girl!* Admittedly, that's an oversimplification. Bella's decision is complex, and Meyer provides all sorts of interesting conflicts and potential consequences. Still, the fact that Meyer makes the vampires and their lifestyle so alluring intrigued me. I couldn't help wondering how vampires changed from revolting parasites to the equivalent of immortal benevolent supermodels, beings with whom almost anyone would gladly spend eternity.

As soon as I began to research vampires, I realized the answer to my question could not seriously be answered in an essay. There's just such a wealth of vampire information—it's even become an academic subject, taught in universities—that there's no way I can properly sum it up here. There are also countless vampire novels adding to the lore, with more showing up in the bookstores every day. Teenage vampires, thanks in part to the success of Meyer's books, seem to have become an industry of their own. Still, with apologies for making sweeping generalizations, I think it's worth looking at some of the sources of these sexy blood-drinkers in order to see just what Meyer has done and perhaps understand how vampires have become so desirable.

A Greatly Abbreviated History of Vampires

According to the *Oxford English Dictionary*, the word vampire didn't appear in English until 1734. But undead creatures who feed on the living have been with us for millennia in one form or another. A great deal of vampire lore is rooted in ancient beliefs in demons, witches, and ghosts. In their most basic form, the stories of these restless spirits were about our connection with the dead—and our difficulty severing that connection. Death has always been the great unknown, feared by most mortals. Whether or not death is truly the end of the individual human spirit is still a subject of debate. It's also a question that is central to nearly every religion. First sweeping generalization: Most religions have some belief in the spirit continuing on, whether it's in Heaven or Hades or Valhalla or through a series of reincarnations. One approach to death, found in many ancient cultures, was ancestor worship, the belief that the spirits of the ancestors remained accessible, watching over those on Earth much like guardian angels. Ritual offerings were made to the dead, encouraging them to protect and bring divine blessings to the living.

The flip side of these helpful spirits of the dead were those harmful to the living, and they were everywhere. Nancy Garden's *Vampires* cites a number of examples, beginning with the ancient Chaldeans, who lived 500 years before Christ and created charms against vampire-like monsters. Garden also describes the Assyrian and Babylonian belief in the Ekimmu. An Ekimmu was the spirit of a person who'd been buried without the proper offerings of food for the afterlife, leaving the spirit eternally hungry. These starving spirits then fed on the living, causing entire families to sicken and die. In Hebrew lore, Lilith was a female demon who was believed to have been Adam's first, disobedient wife and was said to suck the blood from infants and adults. In ancient Sicily and Greece, vampires were the dead who came back for vengeance. If a murderer had not been caught, the victim returned as a vampire, haunting his living relatives until they took proper revenge; if they didn't, they too would be turned into vampires. In the Ukraine and parts of Russia, evil sorcerers and wizards were believed to take the form of vampires so they could feed on the blood of the living. In ancient Ireland, "red-blood suckers" could only be kept in the grave by covering it with heavy stones. Blood, which was equated with the life force, was often key in these tales, but not always. There were also creatures who are now referred to as "psychic vampires." A Korean Tai Chi master once explained to me that according to traditional Korean lore, if a husband died young, it was believed that his wife was a vampire who had killed him, not by taking his blood, but by draining his *chi*, his life force. It seems the most essential component of vampirism is the parasitic feeding on the living.

Second sweeping generalization: Our current crop of the undead seem to be descendants of the Balkan or Slavic vampire beliefs that sprang up in an area that now includes Bosnia and Herzegovina, Romania, Hungary, Croatia, Albania, Greece, Serbia, and parts of Turkey. The borders and names of the countries were somewhat different in the eighteenth and nineteenth centuries when these legends spread, but the entire area was referred to as the Balkans. In the early 1700s, this area went through a frenzy of vampire sightings, with many reported vampire attacks. It's now believed that all of these supposed vampire sightings can be explained by other things that were fairly common 300 years ago, including premature burial (i.e., declaring someone dead when they were merely unconscious); wasting or blood-connected illnesses (e.g., tuberculosis, hemophilia, and porphyria); rabies-induced madness; and superstition. While the vampire's victims were believed to become emaciated and quickly waste away, the vampires themselves were said to become fat with blood, their veins so swollen with what they consumed that blood leaked out of their pores. Whether or not these reports were based in fact, they were considered credible, and they had very real effects on society. Elaborate rituals to identify and control vampires emerged. All sorts of creatures were suspected of vampirism, including butterflies and people who talked to themselves, and the methods for keeping them away often involved garlic, holy water, or crosses. According to Lewis Spence's *An Encylopaedia of Occultism*, there was one sign of vampirism considered absolutely foolproof: unearthing a coffin and finding that the body inside had "wide-open eyes, ruddy and life-like complexion and lips, and a general appearance of freshness, showing no signs of corruption." And so a great many coffins were dug up, their contents staked and beheaded and/or burned to prevent further bloodletting. There was so much of this insanity going on that between 1730 and 1735 there was said to be a vampire epidemic in the Balkans. According to Wikipedia, the Empress Maria Theresa of Austria finally sent her own physician to check out these stories. The good doctor concluded that vampires were just superstition, and Maria Theresa then passed laws that forbade the desecration of graves.

Early Vampire Novels

Though the vampire epidemic never spread to Great Britain, enough of these reports made their way there to inspire two highly influential nineteenth-century novels: John Polidori's *The Vampyre* (1819) and Bram Stoker's *Dracula* (1897). Polidori's novella is said to be based on a fragment of a story[1] by the poet George Gordon, Lord Byron. It's also believed that Polidori, who was Byron's physician, based his vampire villain on Byron himself. Near as I can tell, Polidori's vampire, Lord Ruthven, is the original blueprint for all of the romantic vampires who've followed. Strangely enough, our current notion of the charismatic and sexy undead really began with a notorious British poet.

Byron was, in the early 1800s, the equivalent of a badly behaved rock star. A born aristocrat, he was a magnetic rebel who traveled with a menagerie of animals and led a life that scandalized Europe. His public readings were sold-out events. He appeared at society parties, pale and dressed in black. Men considered him a champion of freedom. Women, especially those who'd never met him, found him irresistible. Lady Caroline Lamb described him in her diary as "mad, bad, and dangerous to know." He was as renowned for his many disastrous love affairs as he was for his poems. (A bisexual,

---

[1] Byron's fragment doesn't really describe the character of the vampire, except to note that he's moody.

Byron was most famously involved with a number of upper-class women as well as his maid and quite possibly his half-sister Augusta.) Byron, like many contemporary celebrities, had an image problem. The real Lord Byron, who was known to be generous, witty, and charming, was often confused with the heroes of his ballads, who were rude, aloof, cynical, and moody.

Like Byron, the vampire Ruthven travels widely, gambles freely, and breaks hearts wherever he goes. He lives with a ruthless disregard for others, which is both condemned as cruel and romanticized as the ultimate freedom. Though Byron was, in his time, simply what we would call a superstar, in Polidori's story this kind of personal magnetism and power are explained as supernatural evil.

Ruthven is an oddly compelling mix of the beautiful and the weird. Although he's described as having a classically handsome face, his skin has a deadly pallor, and he has one "dead grey eye." He also has unusual charm, the ability to deceive men and women alike, and a kind of psychic power over his victims. In one major way Ruthven is the opposite of Meyer's Edward: he delights in ruining the virtue of his victims. In fact, Polidori's vampire tale really seems to be about how the naïve are hoodwinked by evil. Blinded by their own innocence, they're doomed.

Polidori's hero is Aubrey, a young English noble who becomes ensnared by Ruthven's charisma and winds up traveling with him. In Greece, Aubrey falls in love with Ianthe, a young woman who warns him about vampires. Though Aubrey realizes that Ruthven fits Ianthe's description of the undead, he ignores her warnings, and Ruthven, predictably, kills Ianthe. Aubrey remains inexplicably dense. Even after Ianthe's death, he continues to travel with Ruthven until they're attacked by a band of robbers and Ruthven is mortally wounded. Lord Ruthven makes two strange dying requests that Aubrey agrees to: to not tell anyone of his death for a year and a day; and to set his body on a mountaintop in the moonlight. Sure enough, the moonlight heals Ruthven's wounds and he rises from the dead. It doesn't take long before Ruthven appears in England, where Aubrey's own sister falls in love with him and declares that they're going to marry. Aubrey, bound by his own vow, can't tell her of Ruthven's death; he can only warn against the wedding. His sister refuses to heed the warning, and poor Aubrey becomes so frustrated and furious that he wastes away and then dies of a burst blood vessel. His foolish, stubborn sister becomes Ruthven's prey and finally becomes a vampire herself.

Though Polidori's story may now strike us as melodramatic and slightly ridiculous—how could Aubrey be so stupid?—it was incredibly popular in its day and marked the beginning of what became a British vampire craze. Suddenly, other vampire novels and plays began to appear. The most enduring of these was Bram Stoker's *Dracula*. His villain, Count Dracula, was loosely based on the fifteenth-century Transylvanian warrior known as Vlad the Impaler, who was famous for impaling his enemies on spikes. Stoker's Dracula embodies what I think of as the original sense of a vampire: a character who is thoroughly sinister and quite creepy. The story opens with a letter from Jonathan Harker, a young Englishman who's been sent to Dracula's remote castle in Transylvania to help the count purchase some English real estate. Like many of our current vampires, the count is wealthy, exotic, and has mysterious psychic powers. But he is not handsome or remotely attractive, and there is absolutely nothing benign about him. He approaches young women as they sleep, lures them from their beds, drains them of their blood, and leaves them pale and wasted. Eventually they die, but unless a stake is driven through the heart of the corpse and the head is cut off, the dead will leave the grave at his summons and continue the pattern of feeding on the living. Though the count is not what anyone would consider a heartthrob, there's an unmistakable sexual element in his power. When Jonathan Harker first stays in his castle, he enters a forbidden room and encounters three beautiful, voluptuous women, who begin to seduce him, licking their lips then Jonathan's neck. A furious Dracula calls them off before they actually get to bloodletting, because he needs Jonathan's legal services. Jonathan continues to experience eerie things in the count's castle, including a grieving mother who demands that the count return her missing child. Then the count himself undergoes a change. Jonathan finds him in the castle's chapel, lying in a coffin, mysteriously transformed from an elderly man to one who seems half his age. His flesh is bloated and bloodstained, and his face is set in a mocking smile. Harker manages to escape the vampire's castle, but Dracula eventually arrives in England, and his presence is soon felt. Mina Harker (Jonathan's wife) has a good friend named Lucy who mysteriously sickens and dies. Mina then becomes Dracula's next victim.

Stoker's novel holds up well; it's a good, suspenseful story. And though its villain, Dracula, isn't exactly sexy (at least not in contemporary terms), he's compelling and unforgettable. It's easy to read the novel and see how it gave rise to Bela Lugosi's portrayal in the 1931 movie and all of the cinematic spawn who've followed. Stoker's monster lures beautiful young women from their beds, makes them lose all interest in their loved ones, drives them mad, gradually drains them of life, then turns them into monsters. He's a perfect example of the exotic, inscrutable stranger whom good girls really shouldn't get involved with. Like Lord Ruthven, he preys on innocents, and like Ruthven, Dracula was on some level a reaction to traditional religious taboos against sex. That is, if you have sex before or outside marriage, you're committing a sin. But if you have sex with a mysterious stranger who is literally irresistible and entrances you with supernatural powers, you can't possibly be blamed for wrongdoing. You're not responsible for your acts; you're an innocent victim. While the nineteenth-century vampire might not have been handsome or what we think of as romantic, he enabled guilt-free fantasies of desire.

The Romance Continues

When you realize that vampires have had humans falling for them at least since Polidori's time, it's not hard to understand how they've become objects of teenage romance. They fit right in with the old romantic idea of love being an overwhelming force that cannot be resisted. A vampire, with all his or her supernatural charm, makes the love seem fated. How could anyone doubt or hold out against it? The vampire lover is the perfect excuse to junk anything resembling reason or logic and simply follow your heart. Meyer cues us in on this tradition of all-consuming love by making Bella a fan of both Shakespeare's *Romeo and Juliet* and Emily Brontë's *Wuthering Heights*. The interesting thing about this literary tradition is that these older stories, though wildly romantic, were written with a tough dose of realism. Neither Romeo and Juliet nor Heathcliff and Cathy lived happily ever after; their overwhelming loves ended in tragedy.

Another element of the idea of the romantic vampire is that nearly all vamps have phenomenal physical power (Dracula could even climb down steep castle walls like a bat). Aside from stakes, holy water, and the little issue of daylight—which Meyer and other writers have found ways to circumvent—there's not much that can stop a vampire. Why are we so attracted to the powerful? Go ask your ancestors. We're talking about an ancient survival instinct found in nearly every species. Attraction to the powerful is rooted in the desire to be safe and to give one's young the best chance to thrive in a hostile world. The feminist in me hates to admit this, but women are hardwired to find strong, powerful males sexy, which is why there are millions of romance novels, to say nothing of movies and TV shows, in which the heroine falls for a guy whose appeal is that he's powerful, even dangerous. And this is even more embarrassing: There's a connected narrative tradition built around the belief that the right woman can somehow "save" a bad boy, that she'll somehow find a way into his savage heart and tame all those dangerous, bloodthirsty instincts—at the very least stopping the dangerous guy from harming her. Danger, which always ups the excitement level, is what makes him so attractive. The potential killer becomes the protector. Of course, in real life this idea can go horribly wrong. Many violent, dangerous guys can never be "tamed," and that violence is turned on the women who fall for them. Interestingly, that doesn't seem to have affected the fantasy at all. One of the magical things about stories is that they allow readers to imagine themselves as *any* of the characters. So one theory about why fictional dangerous guys like vampires are so attractive is that the reader gets to safely imagine that he or she is the character who is so powerful and irresistible—the vampire and not the helpless victim.

It's not that we've lost the macabre, disturbing aspects of vampirism, but since Stoker's time, those aspects have often become muted and reassigned. Like other young adult writers, Meyer keeps the scary stuff but gives it to her bad vampires, in this case James and Victoria, and the truly terrifying Italian vampire clan, the Volturi. Her good vampires, the Cullens, have their off-putting moments—in *Twilight*, Jasper nearly loses control when Bella gets a paper cut[2]—but the reader is always certain that Bella is safe with them.

So, dangerous? Not so much. Instead, over the years these treacherous, compelling creatures have become sympathetic, and this I suspect has a lot to do with the fact that vampires are outsiders. Outsiders, too, have a long tradition of being romantically intriguing. For one thing, by being outsiders they get to break or ignore all the rules, which immediately makes them more interesting than all the "normal" people. And there's a certain loneliness connected with the loner. Heathcliff, for example, was an outsider

---

[2] A side note: As others have pointed out, though Meyer's vampires react dramatically to paper cuts, none of them seem to notice Bella's monthly menstruation.

adopted by Cathy's wealthy father when Cathy and Heathcliff were both children; Cathy felt sorry for the lonely boy and never got over it. Many of our more recent teen vampires[3]—Simon in Annette Curtis Klause's *The Silver Kiss* and Cal Thompson in Scott Westerfeld's *Peeps*—are loners, isolated from the rest of the world by their vampirism. It's clear that without love, they're hurting. Only the right girl (our romantic heroine) can understand and truly love them.

If, as a writer, you make your romantic hero a vampire, you've already got many of the classic elements in place. You've got a guy who is unbelievably powerful and magnetic (which nowadays includes being extraordinarily attractive), yet because of his outsider loneliness is just vulnerable enough to have his undead heart won. You've also got a hero who is both lethal and oddly protective. Perhaps best of all, these romantic outsiders can offer the heroine the ultimate gift: immortality. Meyer skillfully uses all these classic tropes. Edward is beautiful, almost unimaginably powerful, and of course, irresistible. And he's been waiting more than a hundred years to meet his eternal one and only: Bella.

Edward the Perfect

Though Stephenie Meyer is far from the first writer to make a vampire the object of desire, she does it extraordinarily well. She's taken the concept of the sexy, alluring bloodsucker and pushed it to the extreme. In Edward she's created the ultimate romantic hero. He's off-the-charts handsome, strong, graceful, generous, and all-around brilliant. He's been to Harvard. He plays and composes music. He's got a sense of humor. His "family"—that is, the clan of vampires he lives with—is wealthy, gracious, physically stunning, and dedicated

---

[3] For a frequently updated list of teen vampire fiction, see http://www.monster librarian.com/vampiresya.htm.

to doing no harm to humans. And if all that weren't enough, Edward reads minds—except for Bella's.

Edward also happens to be so morally good that he verges on angelic. Yes, he certainly has his dangerous side, but Meyer keeps him so carefully reined in that he is, in fact, safer than any human teenage boyfriend could ever be. Bella (and by extension, the reader) trusts Edward. We know without a doubt that though he's capable of cheerfully tearing apart the evil Victoria, he would never harm Bella. He repeatedly proves himself to be a guardian angel, dedicating not only himself but his entire family to safeguarding her life. He is so protective that he's nearly paternal. Edward has the innate nobility of a medieval knight; he's forever sacrificing his own happiness for Bella's. Thus, it seems completely believable that when Bella asks to be changed into a vampire so that they can be together for eternity, it's Edward who argues against the change, fighting for the humanity she's so eager to discard. Having grown up in the early part of the twentieth century, he's charmingly old-fashioned, insisting on marriage as a precondition for both lovemaking and changing her into a vampire. And he, unlike Bella, fears for her soul. Though Meyer only touches on this in the first three books, I'm guessing that Edward has a strong, almost religious sense of innocence and sin that may even extend to a belief in Heaven and Hell. He is, in an extremely attractive way, an advocate for chastity, restraint, and moral virtue.

Edward is kin to Polidori and Stoker's nineteenth-century vampires, who allowed readers to safely imagine being caught in an overwhelming attraction that vanquishes all of society's rules. For Polidori and Stoker, however, these were always fatal attractions. Which also makes Edward the complete opposite of those earlier bloodsuckers in that he protects the heroine's honor and her life. Perhaps the way that Edward is most like the classic vampires is that he's consuming on a psychic level. From the moment Bella meets him, she's fixated on him and his unearthly family. She can't stop thinking about them, can't help being drawn to them. This, we find out, is no accident. The vampires' beauty and grace are survival tools, the means by which they lure their victims. Even when Edward does his supernatural best not to harm Bella—he tries to erase himself from her life—he continues to consume her. As Jacob later says, Edward is her drug. She's addicted. Although she can remain alive without him, she's numb, just going through the motions.

I've got to admit, I find it kind of hilarious that Edward and Bella manage to get through three books of 500-plus pages without doing much more than some passionate kissing, despite the fact that they're obsessed with each other from the instant they meet. The books are a fantasy about a compelling yet completely safe, nonsexual relationship. Which is a fascinating progression from Counts Ruthven and Dracula. Those early vampires were figures who, though macabre and evil, were symbols of unrestrained desires. Meyer's Edward exists at the opposite end of the spectrum. Edward is a vampire who is so close to angelic that he becomes a portrait of temptation and unrequited longing. Despite the differences, all three of these vampires present the same risk: Give in to temptation (and sex), and you risk becoming a monster, destroying everyone you've ever loved. Meyer is working not only within the conventions of the classic Victorian vampires, but within their moral framework.

Bella the Vulnerable

Here's another admission. Much as I enjoyed these books—and I read straight through the first three, not wanting to put them down—there were times when Bella got on my nerves. In Polidori's novel, the victims are all innocents, naïve to the point of stupidity. In Stoker's portrait of Mina Harker, however, we get a highly intelligent and independent young woman who manages to effectively fight the vampire even as she realizes that he's draining her blood. Meyer's Bella is a strange blend of a feisty, contemporary teen and two much older stereotypes: the girl who is in nearly continuous need of rescue, and the girl who becomes so addicted to a guy that she literally has no life without him. There were times, especially in *New Moon* before Edward's return, when I just wanted to shake Bella and say, "Get a life, already!"

But the point is that Meyer has given us a heroine who doesn't really have or want a life. When we first meet Bella, she's floating, curiously free of the usual attachments. She certainly doesn't have anything approaching "normal" parent-child relationships. She's always been the caretaker, first for her flighty mom, then for her uncommunicative dad. Though Bella loves her parents, she has no true family and she doesn't seem to have or make any close friends (Cullens aside). She's never felt as if she fit in anywhere. She's an outsider, just waiting for something that feels as if it's truly hers.

Bella is also strangely lacking in passions of her own. She doesn't seem to have any of the usual interests—sports, music, fashion, movies, computer games, politics, etc. She's never been in love. Although she's obviously smart, she doesn't even seem particularly set on going to college. Edward keeps telling her she's extraordinary, yet you have to wonder: What, aside from her scent, is so extraordinary about Bella? I can only think of one thing.

From the start she has a remarkable tendency to put others ahead of herself. Bella is unusually self-sacrificing, especially for a seventeen-year-old. She uproots herself from her home and the one parent she's close to, and she moves to a strange town with a father she barely knows, all because she wants her mother to have a chance at happiness. Near the end of *Twilight*, believing both parents are in jeopardy from James, Bella doesn't hesitate for second. She's more than willing to die, because she believes it will keep her parents (and the Cullens) safe. Long before she decides that she wants to be changed into a vampire, she's ready and willing to give up her own life, and this, I find, is perhaps the strangest thing about Bella. It's also, oddly, one of the most attractive. Bella's willingness to make sacrifices for Edward and those she loves is part of what makes her heroic instead of simply stubborn and perverse.

Meyer gives us a heroine who starts off with deliberately loose ties to family and friends. She arrives in Forks with no real connections. She's not only ripe for the picking but curiously selfless. Leaving this new life (one she's never much liked or been attached to) for the chance of immortality with Edward and the Cullens is on one level a repeat of what she's already done—but this time something's in it for her. The Cullens offer a perfect ready-made family. Adoring, grateful parents who are never restrictive, angry, or punitive but only want you to be happy. Siblings who are similarly wonderful and gorgeous. And they live in a beautiful, spacious house—the diametric opposite of Charlie's depressing, shabby little place—and drive excellent cars. And oh yeah, "changing" means she will no longer be a "danger magnet," always in peril. Instead, she might be able to be with Edward forever. Choosing to give up her life and join the Cullens seems like a no-brainer.

If I had a friend who told me she was giving up her life and humanity to be with her undead boyfriend, I would undoubtedly think she was nuts. But Bella's story is clearly fiction, and because Meyer is working within the conventions of the grand romantic saga, Bella wanting to make this sacrifice just seems like the inevitable, ultimate romantic gesture. After all, Romeo and Juliet willingly gave their lives for each other. And besides, it makes for a highly intriguing plot: Will she or won't she change? Can she really give up dear, sweet Jacob and her family?

Edward and Bella and Us

So we've got a vampire who has been purged of all negative and scary traits to the point of perfection. And we've got a heroine who's strong enough to know her own heart and yet is in constant need of rescue, and is completely addicted to a guy to the point that she really has no life without him. Meyer makes a strong case for Bella's obsessive love. It's easy for the reader to identify with Bella's inability to accept anything other than eternity with Edward.

Still, though Edward could hardly be safer or more appealing, there's something in Bella's insistence on becoming a vampire that I find genuinely creepy. I can buy her wanting to be with Edward forever, and I can buy her being willing to give up living with Charlie, especially if it means moving in with the Cullens. Where I get stuck is with Meyer's repeated emphasis on the Cullens being so ethereally gorgeous and eternally young and Bella's resulting belief that she has to be equally beautiful in order for Edward to truly desire her. She can't help but contrast his spectacular beauty with her own ordinary humanity, and that comparison guarantees that she and Edward will never be equals. She will always be less than—unworthy. This leads to a near-pathological insecurity in the relationship and an all-too-common self-loathing:

> The last was the picture of Edward and me standing awkwardly side by side. . . . The contrast between the two of us was painful. He looked like a god. I looked very average, even for a human, almost shamefully plain. I flipped the picture over with a feeling of disgust.

In the third book, Bella's desire to be changed into a vampire takes on a new desperation triggered by her upcoming birthday. She's worried about turning nineteen while "seventeen-year-old" Edward will never age. This idea of getting older, and particularly of being older than Edward, is more horrific for her than the idea of becoming a bloodsucker. Meyer never really questions this assumption; she just presents this as one of Bella's truths: *It's bad to get old and even worse to look that way.* I might not find this idea so disturbing if it didn't seem to so accurately reflect the society around us. Third sweeping assumption: America is collectively terrified of getting old. It's almost too obvious to say that few people want to look middle-aged, and no one wants to look as if they're over forty. We seem increasingly unwilling to show any signs of age, and the proof is that we spend enormous amounts of money, time, and effort in order to maintain the *appearance* of youth. (Think plastic surgery, breast implants, cosmetic peels, Botox injections, hair weaves and dyes, and expensive "anti-aging" formulas. According to reporter Alex Kuczynski in her book *Beauty Junkies*, the American beauty industry is worth *$15 billion*.) It's something that everyone seems to almost unconsciously agree on: Looking young is not only good and desirable but necessary, at almost any cost. The underlying agreement is that aging and the later stages of life are not good. The problem with all this is that unlike vampires, no matter what we do to our appearance, we *won't* stay young. We will continue to age. It's the consolation prize for not dying. And there is genuine beauty in aging, though it takes a different set of priorities to see it. In many societies, the elders were revered, valued for their experience and knowledge. They were the ones given the ultimate respect. Though it's still this way in certain families, American society as a whole seems to have lost that perspective.

Instead, we seem to be buying in to a wholesale denial of age. We equate getting older with frailty, ugliness, and senility. Bella is not only terrified of looking as ancient and withered as her Gran, she can't bear the idea of being *two years older* than Edward. She's taken our warped attitude toward age and made it even more extreme, and because Bella is so easy to identify with, I can't help but feel uneasy with this. Life *is* change. What Bella's so eagerly signing up for is everlasting stasis.

I have to admit that fear of aging isn't totally unreasonable. The idea of getting old scares me, too. But I find the idea of *not* aging perverse. To me, the difficult but necessary trick is to face things as honestly as possible. Yes, if we're lucky enough to get old—and it is a privilege to be able to survive to old age—then we're on that downward slope toward death. That in itself, though, is not bad. It's simply what being mortal means.

If you study mythology, it becomes clear that the desire for immortal, beautiful youth didn't originate in the last hundred years. Almost every culture has a story involving a magical elixir that guarantees eternal youth. But it's only recently, thanks to the wonders of things like cosmetic surgery and Botox, that unchanging physical perfection seems to be not only within reach but expected. It's the image that's presented to us in nearly every advertisement and in the casting of most TV shows and movies. Certainly, models and movie stars have always been glamorized versions of reality. Airbrushed photos and cosmetic surgery were in vogue well before the twenty-first century, but it seems to me that it's only in the last ten years that this kind of alteration of the body has become mainstream. Bella is squarely part of that mainstream. In wanting to be a vampire, she wants to share the Cullens' gracious family, elegant lifestyle, and their tremendous, fierce power. But most of all, she wants Edward, and she will never fully believe Edward loves her until she shares the vampires' perfect beauty. She never even allows for the possibility that Edward might be right, that he might desire her at any age no matter what she looks like. And she never allows for the possibility that beauty can be something other than physical perfection. In the nineteenth century, vampires were figures of revulsion. In the twenty-first century, it's the normal human condition that repulses.

Don't get me wrong. I enjoyed Stephenie Meyer's books. They've got engaging characters, great pacing, and perfect romantic plot twists. They're a lot of fun. What I've come to see about vampires, though, is that they change with the time and culture they appear in. They're mirrors of our fears and desires. Early bloodsucking vampires were all about the hold that the dead had on the living. It was sort of a reverse of the obvious: that the survivor was clinging to the deceased. Instead, those early vampire tales insisted that it was the dead who couldn't let go. In either case there was a truth in it, that the death of someone you loved could drain the life from you. The stories of psychic vampires told of people who fed on others' energy, drawing their strength from weakening those around them. You often see this sort of thing in cliques, where the alpha girl's status (and power) depends on her having followers weaker than she is. Even Bram Stoker's *Dracula* has been interpreted as a reflection of fears of its time: of foreign influence threatening British society, of our animal nature threatening to overwhelm our reason, and of illicit and irresistible sexual compulsion threatening marriage.

Meyer's vampires—or more accurately Bella's obsession with Edward—seem to mirror our current terror of aging, our own deep fear that without flawless physical beauty, we'll never truly be worth loving. So I find myself wishing that Edward wasn't quite so perfect, and that it wasn't quite so easy to empathize with Bella's willingness to trade her own life for the possibility of that perfection.

● ● ● ● ●

Ellen Steiber is a writer and editor who lives in Tucson, Arizona. Her most recent essays appeared in *The World of the Golden Compass*, edited by Scott Westerfeld, and *Demigods and Monsters*, edited by Rick Riordan. She thanks Eve Sweetser, scholar and friend, and her editor, Leah Wilson, for all the tremendously helpful brainstorming. Ellen's Web site is www.ellensteiber.com.

As Time Goes By

The Heartache of Monster Love

K. A. Nuzum

It ain't easy being a monster. I mean, you look weird. Might even be ugly (unlike darling Edward, of course). You also act strange, and most people notice little quirks like imbibing blood or transforming into a supersized wolf. No wonder most monsters choose to live in relative isolation. The Cullens and the Quileute werewolves hang out in covens and packs, but you can't argue that they're not monsters. For one thing, without supernatural interference, they will never die. Nor will they experience the milestones that define our individuality as humans—special moments in every person's history that create unique memories. K. A. Nuzum says these experiences, coveted by vampires and werewolves alike, are where the tension between Bella and her favorite monsters begins.

As *New Moon* opens on the morning of her eighteenth birthday, Bella is dreaming of her grandmother—her dear, old, wrinkled grandmother. Edward—beautiful, youthful Edward—saunters into the scene, and Bella is faced with having to tell her grandmother she loves a vampire—and she thinks *that's* the disturbing part of the dream. But suddenly, Bella realizes:

> There was no Gran.
> That was me. Me in a mirror. Me—ancient, creased, and withered.
> Edward stood beside me, casting no reflection, excruciatingly lovely and forever seventeen.

Tick Tock

Forever seventeen. Two simple words, and yet they're the source of continuing, unending heartache for Bella and Edward. The fact is, Bella's growing up. She has already passed seventeen, just completed her eighteenth year of life, and is now zipping along toward nineteen. After growing up comes growing old, and in the framework of Edward's eternal life, Bella's eightieth birthday is really just the blink of an eye away.

At least that's the way it feels to Bella, because she lives in historic time—that is, time that passes, that speeds along from one moment to the next from birth to death. Historic time can't be slowed down or stopped or repeated. It has a beginning, a middle, and an end for each of us. The choices that we mortals make in this "time zone" really matter, because they influence what happens to us next. In extreme instances, our choices can even determine how close we find ourselves to the end of our lives, the end of our personal historic time.

For Bella and all of us humans, time proceeds in a straight line, like those moving walkways they have at airports. Instead of taking us to gates 29–41, though, it takes us from birth to death. It has already transported Bella from baby fat to curves and is now whizzing her toward wrinkles. As long as she remains human, she has no choice but to keep moving forward in time. Forward, ultimately, to the end of her life. One of the ironies of our existence is that living means always moving closer to death. There isn't any way to stop the walkway and continue to exist. Or is there?

Make It a Double

Enter the monster. The walkway grinds to a halt when a human is transformed into a monster, and the former human then remains forever at the phase of life in which he or she was at the instant he or she was transformed. So Edward really *is* forever seventeen—without the help of Botox or the International Date Line or time travel, because that's how old he was when he became a vampire.[1] Edward is not going to change or age, no matter what decisions he makes. If Edward smokes, he's never going to get lung cancer. Even if he drinks heavily for 200 or even 250 years, he doesn't have to worry about cirrhosis of the liver. Choices that are land mines for humans don't make a lick of difference to Edward's health or longevity. He is not affected by the ticking of the clock, by the passing of the seasons, by the turning of centuries, because Edward is a monster.

Walking the Walk—What It Takes to Be a Monster

When it comes to pointing a finger and crying "Monster!" people have always been trigger-happy. Pretty much any individual or group that is disliked or viewed as threatening in some way can be and has been monstracized. In various centuries in various cultures, women, the mentally ill, gays and lesbians, Christians, Jews, Muslims, Native Americans, and Blacks have all been labeled as monsters. Even our

---

[1] One of the inconveniences of his eternal youth is that he is forever stuck dissecting frogs year after year in senior biology.

Bella terms herself a monster when she causes emotional pain to other people.

Dictionaries recognize that, more often than not, it is looks and behavior that folks use to identify monsters. In the tenth edition of the *Merriam-Webster Collegiate Dictionary*, the definitions go like this:

> 1a: an animal or plant of abnormal form or structure;
> b: one who deviates from normal or acceptable behavior or character; 2: a threatening force.

So somebody who is icy cold and hard-as-marble like Edward? Clearly monster material. And Jacob Black? Gigantic frame, grows six inches every few weeks, abnormally high temperature, excessive hairiness? Monster!

Behavior-wise, biting people, drinking blood, ripping out throats, eating brains—those are all pretty much universally considered deviant, so their practitioners are typically also labeled as monsters.

There's another behavior that is characteristic of monsters: They tend to establish their headquarters on the outskirts of human population centers. They isolate themselves because it's safer. Maintaining their residences at a discreet distance from people makes them less vulnerable to the prying eyes of humanity, and less likely they will be outed by observant busybody humans who might notice their "abnormal forms" and/or "deviant behavior." That's why, traditionally, vampires inhabited castles on high mountainsides overlooking tiny Romanian villages. And why it was certainly no accident that Dr. Frankenstein's monster was created in the basement of a laboratory atop a barren hill. In our homes, it's one reason kids think monsters are in their dark, messy closets and not skulking around the brightly lit kitchens or lounging on the couch in the living rooms.

This penchant for privacy can be seen among the monsters of the Twilight series as well. The Cullen family lives way off the beaten track, their house so well-concealed it's difficult even to find the turnoff for it. Likewise, the Quileute werewolves live on the reservation of La Push, geographically distinct and removed from the town of Forks. The other group of "civilized" vampires lives way up north in Alaska, which has a small, really spread-out human population.

So far, being a monster is about how you look, how you act, where you live. But even if you're twice as tall as any other human, even if you have an extra toe, enjoy twisted hobbies, and live alone in a cave, you could still be human. If, however, you have all those things going for you *and* people are starting to whisper behind your back about why you still look seventeen but just attended your fiftieth high school reunion, well, my friend, chances are you're a monster. You don't just live in a cave; you live in a different "time zone" than humans do.

The Hamster Wheel

Instead of historic time, monsters abide in mythic time, otherwise known as circular, or eternal, time. If historic time is a moving walkway, mythic time is a hamster wheel. Every day is pretty much the same for a monster. Likewise every year, every century. For monsters of the vampire ilk, the main unchanging, eternally repeating fact of their existence is the thirst for human blood. And that is why the "time zone" they exist in is called circular time. Vampires are stuck forever in the circle of repeating the moment of their own transformation to monster. First they were bitten, which turned them into vampires, then from that moment on, they're all about biting another throat, trying to quench their eternal thirst for human blood.

For all kinds of other monsters, the case is the same. Their own personal historic time ceases at the moment they become a monster, and from there on out, nothing changes for them. They experience an eternal compulsion to commit and recommit the creation act that transformed them into monsters. So while the vampire experiences an unending thirst for human blood, a zombie can't shake the hankering he has for brains, and your traditional werewolf can't rid himself of the burning desire to rip out a human throat when the moon is full.

BRB

Meyer's werewolves aren't traditional. It used to be you could count on a wolfman to show up during a full moon. He had to; every month, when the moon became a bright, round ball in the black sky, like it or not, your cursed human would take on the form of a wolf and go looking to rip out the throat of a human. For the Quileute werewolves, though, the mythic time event that compels their transformation to monster is not the coming of the full moon, but the coming of vampires to tribal lands. When a vampire turns up in the neighborhood, even though a generation or more of time may have passed, the members of the Quileute tribe who carry the werewolf gene find themselves turning into huge, hairy beasts. But these werewolves, instead of being compelled to kill humans, are compelled to protect them.

Meyer has done a bit of waffling in regard to her werewolf monsters: She has given them the ability to exist in mythic time as monsters *and* to reclaim their humanity in historic time.[2] They remain monsters so long as they morph into their wolf forms on a regular basis, and during this time, they are governed by the law of mythic time; they don't change or age. But if they go for an extended period of time without turning into werewolves, they can reclaim their humanity; their clocks start ticking again. As Billy Black explains it in *Eclipse*, "the tribe discovered that the wolf-men could grow old like anyone else if they gave up their spirit wolves."

---

[2] Maurice Sendak does the same thing in *Where the Wild Things Are*.

Ho Hum, Another Rerun

For most monsters, though, the eternal separation of historic time from mythic time is a given. Such will be the case for Bella; as a monster, she'll have an existence of only reruns to look forward to. You'd expect she'd have stronger reservations about joining the group. But from the beginning, unlike most of us, she seems uninterested in experiencing very much of the diversity of love or life available in the human world. Bella tells us soon after we meet her in *Twilight* that she is somewhat alienated from other humans. She says she has a problem relating not just to people her age but to everyone. In the same vein, the girl isn't interested in the events and experiences most of us look forward to having and later on cherishing as memories. Part of the reason we humans place such strong emphasis on marking the milestones of our lives is because they *can't* be repeated or relived. Birthdays, bar mitzvahs, and weddings are unique events that represent particular moments in time, in *our* time. Even though we can't stop our moving walkway, by celebrating special events we capture them, photo-like, and memorialize them.[3]

The Other Side of the Coin

Edward, though, is a different story. You know that saying, "You don't know what you've got till it's gone"? Well, that's Edward all over. As a former human being who can't ever grow up to enjoy the pleasures or accept the responsibilities or revel in the successes of an adult in historic time, Edward realizes how precious those things are. And he wants them for Bella. Although Edward is resigned to his

---

[3] One of the major events of life that Bella will forfeit by moving into mythic time is the possibility of becoming a mother. The only way she will ever be able to bring someone "new" into the world is by creating a monster.

fate, he doesn't want Bella following him into mythic time. He is every bit as obsessed with keeping Bella human as Bella is obsessed with becoming a monster. From the moment they meet, Edward strives to keep her safe. At first he does this by avoiding her, growling at her, trying to keep her at a distance. When he finds he absolutely cannot stay away from her, he gives her verbal warnings that he's not good for her, that having him as a friend is dangerous for her. When she's about to be run down by her classmate's car in the school parking lot, Edward, with his incredible vampiric speed, jumps between her and the car and saves her life. And that moment really begins his campaign to preserve her existence and make certain she gets the most out of it. He drags Bella to prom against her wishes, and even his family gets caught up in marking her eighteenth birthday with a big party:

> He sighed, his lovely face serious. "Bella, the last real birthday any of us had was Emmett in 1935. Cut us a little slack, and don't be too difficult tonight. They're all very excited (*New Moon*).

Of course, the birthday party almost turns into Bella's funeral, what with Bella's paper cut and Jasper's thirst. And it is the final straw for Edward; he quits vacillating and commits to the conviction that his and Bella's monster/human love is doomed. There is no way mingling Bella's vulnerable historic existence with his mythic, eternal existence can lead to anything but her death—her permanent, no-existence-at-all-in-any-way-shape-or-form, "yer oooouuuuuut!" death. Edward understands that the only way life in historic time can be safeguarded is for it to remain distinct and separate from life that exists in mythic time because the monsters of mythic time are driven to destroy the creatures of historic time. And so Edward leaves to keep her safe, ostensibly forever.

Death Threats

Most of us agree with Edward that historic time is a very big deal. We know our time here is limited, that life is temporary, and that there's no such thing as a "do over." And if we die, *when* we die, that's it; we're out of the game. Knowing all of that makes life really, really precious to us. That's why we can't help feeling a bit torn about Bella becoming a monster and giving up her time as a human. What we do know for sure, though, is that we don't want her to just be dead. If she's going to leave her place in historic time, we want her to at least be able to continue on in mythic time, and we want her to do it with Edward at her side.

So we get very tense when it looks like, time after time in the series, a monster might end Bella's human life *and* steal her opportunity for monsterhood with Edward. Did you notice that the preface in each book features a threat to Bella's life by a monster? This is what pulls us into all of the novels so quickly and keeps us turning pages, wondering: Will Bella die?

> I'd never given much thought to how I would die—though I'd had reason enough in the last few months—but even if I had, I would not have imagined it like this.
>
> I stared without breathing across the long room, into the dark eyes of the hunter, and he looked pleasantly back at me.

That's from the preface of *Twilight*, where even before we know who the protagonist is, we are hooked because a human life is in jeopardy. And we realize from the get-go that what threatens this life is something other than human. The threat is a "hunter," so it could be an animal, but it "looks pleasantly back," which only a person would do. Lightbulb goes on: Monster!

All three books are filled with these threats to Bella's historic existence at the hands—er, make that the *teeth*—of monsters, some well-intentioned, most of them just plain nasty. There's the time Jasper almost puts the bite on Bella at her birthday party, and the time Laurent finds Bella alone in the clearing where the Cullens played baseball, and of course, the example from *Twilight's* preface: James luring her to the dance studio.

For this reader, James represents the cruelest and most horrifying threat of all. How come? As a vampire, James has, in Alice's words, "a glut of weapons . . . the strength, the speed, the acute senses," and "like a carnivorous flower" is "physically attractive to . . . prey" (*Twilight*). But horribly, monstrously, instead of his supernatural powers, he chooses to use Bella's humanity as bait and trap for her. He manipulates human love and the human impulse to protect others to achieve his monstrous ends. Although far from human, James nonetheless understands that to a human heart, love for another is a treasure above all others. A beloved person is worth protecting and worth the sacrifice of one's own time in history. James knew that Bella would give her life to safeguard her mother's.

S'all Good

This profound emotional commitment to life that we all feel helped Stephenie Meyer hook us on her stories. But, it also presented her with a problem she had to overcome. Knowing we are temporary beings in this world, we tend to keep a stranglehold on life until the very end, and naturally, we want all other good guys to do the same. The Cullen family members are definitely good guys, and we are genuinely fond of them, so Meyer had to find a way to make readers feel okay about all of them having traded their mortal lives for stone-cold, hamster-wheel monsterhood. The author accomplished this tricky feat by drawing the human existences of Cullen siblings and parents as horribly tragic and/or completely doomed. And she did it so dramatically that we actually feel grateful there was an alternate path of existence available to them. So we have Edward just hours away from expiring in the 1918 Spanish flu pandemic, with not only his mother's blessing but her *command* that Carlisle save her son; Alice, who spent most of her human existence caged in a dark, dank asylum cell because of her ability to see the future; Emmett, like Edward about to expire, but at the paws of a marauding bear; and Esme, so broken by the death of her child that she could bear life in this world no longer.

She Loves Me, She Loves Me Not

Jacob is another who can no longer bear the pain of loss that is always a part of life in historic time. In Jacob's case, it is the anguish of losing Bella to and for eternity. During Edward's prolonged absence, Jacob falls in love with Bella and begins to nurture a hope for building a life with her in historic time, a hope for marriage, children, a whole lifetime together. But, upon Edward's return, his hopes are crushed, for even though Jacob can live life in historic time, Bella is determined not to. At the end of *Eclipse*, after Edward has convinced Bella to both graduate from high school and marry him before he transforms her into a monster, we watch Jacob escape into mythic time, and our hearts break right along with his. We grieve his ruined dreams for love in historic time, and we grieve the loss of the human Jacob Black:

> If the silence in my head lasted, I would never go back. I wouldn't be the first one to choose this form over the other. . . . I pushed my legs faster, letting Jacob Black disappear behind me.

Forever Seventeen

> It changes everything about them. In that instant
> when they shift from one form to the other, they don't
> really even exist. The future can't hold them . . .
> (*Eclipse*).

Although that is Edward's description of a Quileute transforming
into a werewolf, it holds true for humans becoming monsters of any
kind. The moment of transformation from human to monster is the
instant in which one loses his or her unique place in historic time,
the instant in which one's moving walkway stops forevermore.

The heartache of monster love is defined by that moment, when
the experience of time for human beings diverges sharply from the
experience of time for monsters. This unbridgeable difference is a
huge source of pain, uncertainty, and indecision for Edward and
Bella.

The reality of the incompatibility of their "time zones" creates a
lot of tension and suspense for the reader too. Throughout the series,
we wonder over and over again if Bella will sacrifice her one and
only opportunity to live a long, full human life to take on the existence of a bloodthirsty, ice-cold, hard-as-marble monster trapped
forever in mythic time, and we turn page after page hoping to discover the answer. Even over the course of three books and almost
2,000 pages, the question holds us spellbound because it is such a
profound one for us; our ability to experience the passing of time is
at the core of what it means to be human. It is our experience in time
that defines us as individuals, that gives meaning and uniqueness to
each of our lives, because the things we do, the choices we make, the
unexpected events that come our way, all of these are different for
each of us. And though we know living means we will eventually
reach our own end, most of us still would not want to give it up,
would not be content to be *forever seventeen*.

• • • • •

K. A. Nuzum is the author of the critically acclaimed novel *A Small White Scar*. Her second novel, *The Leanin' Dog*, will be out in October 2008. K. A. holds an MFA in writing for children and young adults from Vermont College. Sunday afternoons of her childhood were spent glued to the family's television set watching old werewolf and vampire movies starring Lon Chaney, Jr., and Bela Lugosi.

Destination: Forks, Washington

Cara Lockwood

> Ever notice how some of the scariest movies ever made are set in small towns? Ever wonder why some of the creepiest books likewise take place away from big cities? Cara Lockwood says it's because chainsaw-wielding weirdoes would be much too obvious, dismembering their victims in a walk-up apartment. And face it, werewolves need open spaces to lope, while vampires like the Cullens require the kind of anonymity (not to mention big game hunting) found in the middle of nowhere. Forks, Washington, is the perfect setting for the Twilight books. But did you know it's a real place? Lockwood takes you on a tour.

I don't like road trips. And I'll tell you why.

Sure, there's the whole being trapped in a car for hours eating Big Macs for days thing, while your legs go numb and you start wondering if it's possible to die of boredom.

But for me it's more than that.

I could handle death by French fry. What I can't handle is driving by all those small towns.

Some people love small towns. My stepdad grew up on a farm, and he loves taking those winding back roads in the country—the ones lined with cows on either side, and green hills and trees, that have blinking red lights because there's not enough traffic for a single stoplight. Even my mom likes shopping in small towns. She says she finds good antiques there.

But anytime I get away from the city and I find myself far from a major highway on one of those two-lane windy roads with poorly marked signs, I start to get nervous.

Because the fact is I find small towns creepy. If you've ever seen a single horror movie, you know that most of them take place in small towns.

Here's a short list of what you can find in your typical horror-movie small town: chainsaw-wielding psychos, inbred mutant cannibals, vampires (of the not-Edward, not-so-nice variety), vengeful ghosts, evil witches, haunted houses/hotels/entire towns, crazy murderers who've turned the town into wax figures, and on occasion, entire high schools taken over by aliens.

And that's just what happens in movies. There are all those TV shows, too, like *Twin Peaks* and *Smallville*. Did Superman pop up in the middle of Manhattan? Nope. He crash-landed his space pod from Krypton in the middle of a corn field.

Why is it always a small town in those horror movies or TV shows? Part of the reason could be that small towns just make good locations for stories. They're remote, far from big police stations and the FBI.

If Superman had crashed in Times Square, I'm pretty sure the FBI and Homeland Security would've carried him off to Roswell (another small town!), or Area 52, or wherever it is that they do secret government experiments on aliens, and then there would've been no Clark Kent and no story.

The same could be said for the crazed cannibal family of *Texas Chainsaw Massacre* fame. I doubt they could live easily in the Upper West Side of Manhattan. The neighbors would probably complain pretty loudly about that noisy chainsaw, and Leather Face would turn a few heads on the subway no doubt, even in New York.

Whatever the reason, there's just something weird about small towns.

So when I first picked up *Twilight* and read about Bella moving to Forks, I knew something weird was going to happen when she got there. I didn't even need to read the back cover. I just knew.

Because at first, Forks, Washington, seemed like just another weird small town. Was it creepy? Check. Remote? Check. Rainy? Check. Obscure? Check.

Even our beloved narrator Bella Swan doesn't like Forks. She tells us so in the very first pages.

> In the Olympic Peninsula of northwest Washington State, a small town named Forks exists under a near-constant cover of clouds. It rains on this inconsequential town more than any other place in the United States of America. It was from this gloomy, omnipresent shade that my mother escaped with me when I was only a few months old. . . . It was to Forks that I now exiled myself—an action that I took with great horror. I detested Forks.

I felt for Bella right away. Moving to a small town for me would be like a claustrophobic person deciding he or she was going to try out living in an elevator for awhile.

And what weird thing did Bella find once she moved to Forks? Not the old, beat-up Chevy her dad, Forks's Police Chief, gave her. Nope. Naturally, she met some vampires.

Given my suspicion of small towns, it didn't surprise me at all that a family of vampires lived in Forks. What did surprise me was that they were *nice* vampires, and not the bloodythirsty evil kind that pretty much destroyed that tiny Alaskan town in *Thirty Days of Night*.

It made sense on many levels that the Cullens—Edward, Rosalie, Jasper, Alice, and their "parents," Carlisle and Esme—would choose Forks as their residence. The cloud cover and constant rain give them protection. If Edward or any member of his vampire family is seen in the sunlight, their vampire skin sparkles and shines, and it's difficult to keep a low profile looking like a walking disco ball.

Plus, Forks is near dense woods populated with big animals, enough to sustain a family of vampires trying not to eat people. Having wildlife nearby makes hunting bears and cougars a snap. That's not something that would be easy to do if you lived in, say, Pasadena. I don't think they stock bear blood in the juice aisle of the local Stop 'N Shop.

The woods also provide a good place for their remote castle-like home, far from prying eyes.

But even though Edward and his family were nice, I still wasn't won over by Forks.

I don't know about you, but when Bella decided to take a walk into the forest to clear her head after a run-in with Edward, I didn't need him to tell me it was dangerous for her to be wandering around the woods by herself. Anyone who's seen pretty much any B-list horror movie knows that bad things live in the woods.

In a place like Forks, where it always rains (cue creepy music now!), you just never know what might happen. And I was fine with that, because I was reading a book, and the book was fiction, and I wasn't anywhere near Forks or any other fictitious small town.

Except that Forks isn't some made-up town. Forks is a *real* place. It really does exist.

I know because I felt compelled to look it up and find out.

After a brief Web search, I discovered that Forks sits 141 miles west of Seattle, about a four-hour drive. Among some of its tourist attractions are: more than 100 miles of saltwater shores, alpine meadows, and rain forest valleys; 200 miles of wild rivers filled with native salmon; and lots and lots of trees and rain. Yes, it does rain. A lot. Average rainfall is 122 inches a year. That's more than double the national average.

Once known for being the logging capital of the world, Forks is now most famous for being home to Bella Swan and Edward Cullen, not to mention a pack of werewolves and a whole family of other vampires.

You'd think the good people of Forks (all 3,120 of them) would be upset to be seen as one of the world's most famous homes to monsters, next to Transylvania and wherever it was that Franken-stein lived. After all, Stephenie Meyer didn't actually visit Forks before she wrote *Twilight*. She needed a rainy place to hide the Cullen Family, and Forks fit the bill.

I thought most people actually living in Forks might take offense to their town being overrun with monsters. So I decided to interview a few of them to find out.

I headed straight to the city's spokesperson—Nedra Reed, mayor of Forks—to see what she thought.

"On behalf of the community, I can say that we're pleased that Ms. Meyer chose us, even though her reasons were different than the ones we might have chosen," said Reed. "It's been a real boon to the commu-nity. I've run into people in town who were here because of the books. They wanted to come see for themselves what Forks was really like."

In fact, after talking to the mayor a little more and poking around online, I found out that tourists from all over the world have descended on Forks to see some of the actual locations from the books, including Forks High School, where Bella first meets Edward, and La Push, home to the Quileute Indian Tribe and the Twilight series's native werewolf clan.

Visitors have come from as far away as Spain and Germany just to walk in the footsteps of Bella and Edward. And a lot of them head to the Forks Chamber of Commerce Visitor Center.

I called there next.

"Sometime early in 2006 people would come in to the center and say there's this book about Forks," said Mike Gurling, who manages the visitor center. "We had no idea. So then we realized it was really popular. Stephenie Meyer came in July 2006 and did a book signing and people came from all over the country to get signed copies. She had never been to Forks before she wrote *Twilight*, but said that it was a lot like she'd pictured it."

Gurling found so many people pouring into his office asking about *Twilight* that he and his staff finally drew up special maps for out-of-towners looking to see the places mentioned in the book.

Now on the Chamber of Commerce's Web site (http://www. forkswa.com/) you can find a map detailing all the main Twilight series attractions, including pictures of all the major sites. Here are the highlights:

Forks High School

This, of course, is where Bella meets Edward for the first time. There are several meaningful spots on campus, like the cafeteria, where Bella first gets a glimpse of Edward; the classroom where they share a lab table; and, of course, the front office where Bella is almost eaten by Edward. That is, before he manages to get his appetite under control.

Forks Community Hospital

When Bella is nearly killed by a careening car in the school's iced-over parking lot, Edward manages to save her with inhuman speed and strength. To address her relatively minor injuries, she's taken to the local hospital to be treated. There, she's cared for by Edward's "adopted" father, Carlisle.

First Beach

After a few puzzling run-ins with Edward in which Bella comes to believe there's something unusual about the beautiful, pale-skinned boy, Bella accepts an invitation to First Beach from some of her friends from Forks High School. There, she runs into an old family friend, Jacob, a member of the Quileute Indian Tribe. He tells Bella about an old legend of men descended from wolves and their natural enemies, vampires, and how his ancestors made a treaty with the "good" vampires. It's then that Bella starts to put the pieces of the puzzle together and realizes Edward's true nature.

La Push (the Quileute Reservation)

This is where Jacob lives. And where the werewolves roam.

Port Angeles

In the nearby shopping village Bella visits **Gottschalk's,** where she goes to shop for prom dresses with her friends. **Port Books and News** is the bookstore Bella passes alone right before she runs into the group of men who plan her harm. And **Bella Italia** is the restaurant Bella and Edward go to after Edward saves her from her would-be attackers.

Quillayute Prairie Cemetery

This is the place where Edward takes Bella when they decide to watch his family's game of high-speed, high-action vampire base-ball. Of course, the noise attracts a wandering group of three vampires, who then become obsessed with hunting Bella.

And there are some not-so-prominent places you can visit, too:

Forks Police Station

This is the place where Bella's father works. It's mentioned in passing in *Twilight*, but Bella never actually goes here.

Forks Outfitters

This is the only grocery store in town, so Bella would've done all her shopping here. It's never actually mentioned in the book, but Bella did do all the cooking for her dad and we assume all the shopping, too.

If you swing by the visitor's center, you'll get a special *Twilight* packet, including a town map and some actual sand from First Beach.

I decided to e-mail a few people at the high school next, to see if tourists had been banging down the doors to see the location where Bella and Edward first meet. And according to Kevin Rupprecht, principal of Forks High School, a lot of those tourists have.

So what do all the students think about their school being famous?

"To quote a common student sentiment, 'Really, my school?'" said Rupprecht. "I think this is a fairly common thought amongst students. This is their home. They are used to their building, and visitors have an alternative perspective because it is all new to them."

Rupprecht doesn't take issue with how Forks High School is portrayed.

"I think that there are components of *Twilight* that hit fairly close to home for Forks," he said, "but I think the author took enough creative license to make her setting appropriate for the story. Visitors to Forks are sometimes disappointed because they are unable to find various locations mentioned in the text."

Like Bella's house, for example.

"I can't tell you where she lived," Gurling admits. "That's a tough one."

The fact that Bella, Edward, and Jacob aren't real people doesn't mean that visitors don't keep trying to find them. In fact, both Bella and Edward get quite a lot of mail sent to the central Forks post office.

"They both get lots of letters," Gurling says. "But Bella gets the most by far. Although Edward gets some interesting mail, too. In the book, he drives a Volvo, and someone sent him a warranty for a new Volvo."

Despite the fact that Bella and Edward don't really exist, Gurling says the book is pretty accurate about Forks.

"It does rain a lot, that's true," he said. "There were a few minor things that were wrong, like some directions they were driving, but over all, Forks was captured pretty well."

Except, of course, for the fact that vampires and werewolves don't actually roam the streets. Right?

"Not to my knowledge," Mayor Reed said.

But many residents are embracing the fictional characters. The Chamber of Commerce even recently declared Bella Swan's birthday a town-wide holiday.

Of course, technically, the town holiday was originally going to be Stephenie Meyer's birthday.

"But then we found out that her birthday is December 24," said Gurling. "And that would be a tough day to have a big celebration, so we wound up going with Bella's birthday, which is September 13."

The event drew a modest crowd of fans and gave local businesses a chance to sell new merchandise, including T-shirts that say "My last Twilight, I was bitten in Forks, Washington." Even the local police chief (no relation to Bella Swan, by the way) got in on the festivities by making peanut butter sandwiches at the library, where people gathered to eat cake, gobble down snacks, and exchange stories about their favorite scenes in the Twilight series.

Gurling said they hope to make it a regular town holiday, including cake and maybe even a visit from Stephenie Meyer next year.

"We're hoping she'll come," he said. "Her fourth book comes out next fall. It would be great if it was coming out about that time. That would be ideal."

The Twilight fervor is only likely to grow as shooting for the *Twilight* movie begins this spring.

"They're going to be filming the movie this next spring, and the director of the movie was here a month or so ago," Gurling said. "We don't know how much of it will be filmed here. Some will be filmed in Vancouver, British Columbia, but some scenes are going to be here. And since some of it will be in Forks, we won't be surprised if tourism goes up even more after that. We'll not only have the books promoting Forks but also a movie."

So why do so many people in Forks not seem to mind that they're famous for being home to monsters? In part, because the attention comes at a time when many local businesses are struggling. Gurling said that the local economy has been hard hit by slowdowns in the logging industry and by the economy as a whole.

"There's been an economic downturn, and that's true of a lot of small towns," he said. "So increased tourism comes at a great time for us."

And there's not just the scenes from the Twilight series to see in Forks, either.

"I would say people come here now who would not have come here before the books," he said. "But once they're here, I think people are very surprised about the natural beauty that's here. We've got a number of parks and really beautiful points of interest."

So after talking to all these nice people in Forks, I have to admit I was getting a little less nervous about the whole small town thing. Forks sounds like a nice place full of nice people.

Of course, I can say that easily, as I was still safely tucked away behind my computer in the bustling city of Chicago, hundreds of miles away. Despite all the niceness, I still couldn't help but wonder:

Why *do* so many weird things happen in small towns? I decided to ask some of my new friends in Forks.

"You know, one of my theories is that not a lot is known about small towns," Gurling said. "Everybody knows a lot about Los Angeles—like there's lots of smog and traffic there—but not a lot is known about small towns because few people live there and few people know about them. They're mysterious. And because not a lot is known, you can write what you want to write, where your imagination takes you, and people might not immediately discount it."

The school principal said he thinks Forks was picked not because it was a small town, but because Forks makes such a great setting for a story.

"I do not know if small or large makes a difference," he said. "I think that the geography and other setting aspects make the difference. Forks is a picturesque town in a beautiful area."

The mayor said she doesn't have a theory about why Forks was chosen for a book about vampires and werewolves.

"I'm a sixty-five-year-old grandmother," she said. "So those books aren't really my genre. But I am very glad she picked Forks. We all are."

So while you may not find werewolves or vampires on your next trip to Forks, you will find a whole town full of really nice people. And beautiful parks. And a few fellow die-hard Twilight fans.

While I'm not sure if I'm completely over my small town phobia, after talking to the good people of Forks, I am sure of one thing: I wouldn't mind visiting.

• • • • •

Cara Lockwood is the author of the Bard Academy series, published by MTV Books, which includes *Wuthering High*, *The Scarlet Letterman*, and *Moby Clique*. She also is the author of *I Did (But I Wouldn't*

Now), *Dixieland Sushi*, *Pink Slip Party*, and *I Do (But I Don't)*, which was made into a Lifetime Original Movie. She lives with her husband and daughter near Chicago, where she is currently working on her next novel. Visit her online at www.caralockwood.com or www.bardacademy.com.

Dear Aunt Charlotte

Cassandra Clare

When a gossip columnist receives a letter asking whether Edward or Jacob would make the best boyfriend, she understands the question. After all, she's a Twilight fan, too. In search of the answer, she turns to the silver screen. For in the movies, were-wolves and vampires become more than inhuman monsters, despite their despicable deeds. Cassandra Clare (a.k.a. Aunt Charlotte, gossip columnist extra-ordinaire) gives us a rundown, from the 1935 classic *The Wolf Man*, which portrays werewolves as tor-tured souls, to the recent *The Lost Boys*, which pres-ents vampires as party boys. And who would make the best boyfriend? Aunt Charlotte offers her opinion.

Dear Aunt Charlotte,

I have a feeling this is going to be a very unusual sort of letter. You see my problem isn't a real problem; it's fictional. I've always been the sort of girl who gets far too obsessed with books, and right now I'm obsessed with the Twilight series. You may have heard of it—it's the story of Bella, a teenage girl forced to choose between two wonderful guys: her best friend, Jacob, and her boyfriend, Edward. Edward is romantic and wonderful and says things like, "Before you, Bella, my life was like a moonless night." He's even offered to pay for her to go to college next year. Jacob is kind and strong and swears that he loves Bella more than anything. There's something else I should mention: Edward is a vampire, and Jacob is a werewolf, so of course they hate each other, and not just because of Bella. None of my friends can agree on whether Bella should choose to be with Edward or Jacob, and I thought maybe your extensive experience advising people about relationships could help me make up my mind. Who should Bella be with—Edward or Jacob? The vampire or the werewolf?

Yours,
A distraught fan of Twilight

Dear Twilight fan,

Aunt Charlotte is indeed familiar with the books in question, and let me tell you, I understand your distress. It's always hard to choose between wonderful guys, and since fictional men are just better, well, that makes the decision even harder. Aunt Charlotte would also like to note that this kind of question is a nice change of pace, since in books it always seems to be a girl torn between a vampire and a werewolf, unlike in real life when she would be torn between a mailman and an area insurance adjuster named Bob.

The thing about deciding between fictional supernatural men is this: You can't turn to real-life examples to help you solve your dilemma. After all, in the real world perfectly sensitive, perfectly caring teenage boys who also have high cheekbones and luminous golden eyes do not exist. Ahem. What Aunt Charlotte meant to say was that, in the real world, vampires and werewolves do not exist.

So how can we decide what they might be like as romantic partners? Well, by turning to the medium in which they were first depicted as romantic figures: the silver screen.

Years ago vampires and werewolves were seen merely as repulsive, evil monsters. It was in a large part due to their haunting portrayals in such films as *The Wolf Man*, *Dracula*, *The Howling*, *The Lost Boys*, *The Company of Wolves*, and *Buffy the Vampire Slayer* that led to their widespread acceptance as the figures of romantic melancholy they are today. In fact, films have played a huge part in developing our current vampire and werewolf mythology. For instance, the fact that werewolves change shape at the full moon, are allergic to silver, and can be defeated by wolfsbane was first invented in the 1941 film *The Wolf Man*.

The Wolf Man is the tale of an American-educated Englishman, Laurence Talbot, who returns to his ancestral home in Wales to reconcile with his father. He falls in love with Gwen, a local girl, who gives him a walking stick decorated with the silver head of a wolf. She tells him this represents a "werewolf," and recites a local poem:

> Even a man who is pure in heart
> and says his prayers by night
> may become a wolf when the wolfbane [sic] blooms
> and the autumn moon is bright.

Talbot scoffs at the legend, which in horror movies always means you're about to become lunch for a local monster. Sure enough, he's soon bitten while attempting to protect Gwen's friend Jenny from an apparent wolf attack. The curse of lycanthropy is passed along to Larry, who proceeds to prowl the countryside, marauding, until he's beaten to death by the father he came home to reconcile with—ironically, with the silver-headed walking stick Larry got from Gwen.

The Wolf Man presents the wolf as a tormented hero. He's a human being who knows he can't control his transformations into a monster. Werewolves are generally seen as masculine, testosterone-fueled figures, unlike their more foppish cousins, the vampires. (Interesting that a monster so associated with rampant masculinity would be controlled by the moon, a planet usually associated with the feminine. Or perhaps women are the werewolf's weakness?) The werewolf as presented here *wants* to be a good boyfriend—he's a romantic and in love with Gwen—but just can't control his animal side. A love affair with a guy like this would by necessity be fatally flawed—he's a good man who can't stop himself from killing and is therefore doomed.

The werewolf made numerous appearances in film after *The Wolf Man* proved popular, including *The Curse of the Werewolf*, *Werewolves on Wheels*, *The Beast Must Die*, *I Was a Teenage Werewolf*, and the memorably named *Werewolf in a Girls' Dormitory*. Werewolves in these films are rarely portrayed as thinking, feeling creatures, much less romantic heroes. They tend to be rapacious monsters—"the horror of all mankind!" as one movie poster promises—bent on death and bloodshed. Part of this was due to the proliferation of production companies like Amicus and Hammer, who churned out formulaic horror pictures at a remarkable rate that left little time for paying attention to script and character detail. Another part was due to early, crude special effects that made a convincing—and moving—transformation from man into wolf difficult to achieve.

The '80s brought better special effects and a revived interest in werewolves with personality and human feelings. Seminal films like *The Howling*, *An American Werewolf in London*, and *Wolfen* appeared during this decade, challenging the portrayal of werewolves as mindless monsters.

The Howling, released in 1981, is notable not only for its advanced special effects but also for presenting werewolves as sexy and sexual beings. The heroine, hiding out after a traumatic experience with a serial killer, finds herself among a band of werewolves—but these werewolves are comfortable with themselves and their animal natures, unlike the tortured hero of *The Wolf Man*. Touching

on some of the back-to-nature and environmental movements popular at the time, these werewolves are portrayed as in touch with
nature, the earth, and their own sexuality. But while they're sexual,
they're not precisely *romantic*. One gets the sense that these werewolves aren't much with the giving of flowers, or the long walks on
the beach. Their sexuality may be natural, but it's also brutal and
abrupt, and one gets the sense that they'd be just as comfortable eating the heroine as making love to her. In fact, they may have some
trouble telling the difference.

An American Werewolf in London, on the other hand, presents the
werewolf as a regular guy trapped in a nightmare. After being
attacked by a werewolf while backpacking across the Yorkshire
Moors (as anyone who reads Gothic romances knows, nothing good
ever happens on the Yorkshire Moors), young American traveler
David moves in with the beautiful nurse who took care of him in the
hospital. They fall in love, but once the night of the full moon
arrives, David changes into a wolf in a painful and lengthy transformation involving agonizing twisting of flesh and snapping of bones.
But it's nothing compared to the torment David suffers when he realizes he's responsible for the death of a dozen Londoners. He's finally
shot and killed after being lulled into a sense of security by his girlfriend, who tells him she loves him.

Boyfriend factor: not good. David is an ordinary, affable guy by
day, but a vicious and mindless killer by night. He has absolutely no
control over his transformations, nor over his behavior during the
times he's transformed. The brutality of the transformation itself
presages the brutality David shows to everyone he meets while in
wolf form. Romance with a werewolf might be possible if the werewolf were conscious of his actions during the time he's transformed,
or if there were some way of restraining him (à la Oz in the *Buffy the
Vampire Slayer* TV series), but *An American Werewolf in London* does-
n't posit either as a possibility: Lycanthropy here is a disease, like
rabies or syphilis, that takes your will and mind before it takes your

life. David might love the nice nurse, but it's not enough to control his bloodlust.

Teen Wolf sends the opposite message: the werewolf in this film would be a *great* boyfriend. Partly because he is played by Michael J. Fox, who is inherently likeable, and partly because lycanthropy in this version of events seems to have no actual drawbacks. It doesn't make you bloodthirsty, savage, or driven to eat rabbits by the light of the moon. It just makes you hairier, zippier, and better at basketball and dancing to '80s synth pop. While the lycanthrope in this film is charming and eventually gets the girl, he does lack the *animalistic* magnetism we've come to expect from our werewolf boys—he's such a sweet, ordinary guy that he seems a bit anemic (the work of our friend the vampire, perhaps?). One notable thing about this werewolf mythology is that Fox's character is born a werewolf rather than made one through an attack. It's an inherited trait, like male pattern baldness, which may help explain why he adjusts to it so easily and with minimum drama.

Wolfen presents an intriguing picture of the werewolf as a relic of a more natural world. Though the werewolves in the film do kill, often brutally, they're driven by more than appetite: Their first victim is a land developer, someone who's directly responsible for destroying the natural habitat of wolves and driving them into human habitats. These aren't wolves, precisely, but *wolfen*: creatures tied to Native American myths of shapechangers and skinwalkers. Like Jacob in the Twilight series, these werewolves are born what they are, and their shapechanging magic reaches back into their origins in Native American folklore. "Wolves and Indians evolved and were destroyed simultaneously. Their societies are practically one and the same. They're both tribal, they look out for their own, they don't overpopulate, and they're both superb hunters," says one of the characters in the film, making the connection explicit. Now, how romantic are these wolfen as mythic figures? Well, boyfriend-wise, they're kind of like that guy in college who was really dedicated to environmental causes and activism and didn't have a lot of time for romance. These wolves are killers, but that's not really the problem: They're fighting for the continuation of their species and seem entirely dedicated to that purpose. So while they're noble warriors, which can be attractive, they don't seem like they have much time for the opposite sex.

And then there's *Underworld*. You said in your letter that since Edward and Jacob are a werewolf and a vampire, they have "other reasons to hate each other besides Bella." It does seem to be the case that werewolves and vampires are often considered natural enemies, creatures that have hated each other since the dawn of time. And yet in *House of Dracula*, one of the earliest horror films in which both Dracula and the Wolf Man made an appearance, they seem friendly enough, both searching for cures for their supernatural afflictions (only the Wolf Man gets one, and rides off happily into the sunset, perhaps stoking the fires of resentment in his less fortunate colleague). In the later *Abbott and Costello Meet Frankenstein*, the Wolf Man is on hand to warn the comedians of Dracula's nefarious schemes, casting himself as the "good monster" while Dracula is the bad one. Though both these films made use of Universal's more famous horror properties, neither of them gave audiences what they were clearly dying to see: vampires and werewolves fighting each other.

Some vampire legends maintain that vampires fear wolves and that a wolf can be used to keep a vampire at bay. Other legends maintain that a werewolf *becomes* a vampire after death, or that a vampire can take wolf form as well as bat form. No specific legend states that vampires and werewolves dislike each other, but that hasn't stopped Hollywood from running with the idea. In *Underworld*, both lycanthropy and vampirism are caused by a virus—a mutation of a plague, which caused vampirism in a man bitten by a bat and lycanthropy in his brother who was bitten by a wolf. Werewolves and vampires go on to be each other's mortal enemies throughout the centuries, each group dedicated to eradicating the other.

Both the Lycans and the vampires in *Underworld* are portrayed as sexy and attractive in their human forms. The main Lycan, Michael, is a deeply romantic figure: Uncomfortable with his monstrous side at first, he eventually adjusts and becomes a tough and self-possessed warrior. He's handsome, tormented, and in love with a vampire girl named Selene (that her name means "moon" in Latin harks back to Aunt Charlotte's earlier guess that women, like the moon, are a male werewolf's weakness). Would he make a good boyfriend? Probably, if he could get past his need to take part in the endless war raging between vampires and werewolves.

The vampires in *Underworld* would also make excellent boyfriend material if they would just put down the silver bullets for a few minutes and concentrate on the romance. They're also gorgeous—their eyes glow blue, and they wear super-sexy tight leather outfits. They also evince many of the traits we've come to associate with vampires—increased strength and speed and heightened senses and perception, not to mention beauty and charm. They're presented as sophisticated, elegant, and cultured—Darcys to the Lycans' more rough-and-tumble Heathcliffs.

The depiction of vampires as elegant and charming on film is a fairly recent one—in the classic *Nosferatu*, probably the first vampire film ever made, the titular vampire has repulsive, ratlike features and long dirty fingernails. Also his ears are huge. He looks like a cross between a rodent and the World Cup. If he was the vampire clamoring for Bella's affections, she wouldn't have any problem picking the hot werewolf. Nosferatu would *not* make a good boyfriend. It's somewhat unclear in the film if he can even talk, though some might regard this as a plus.

In *Dracula*, released in 1931, we see the first emergence in film of the vampire as steamy upper-class seducer. His slow and deliberate speech patterns, his unnerving glowing stare (the cinematographer shone pinpricks of light into his eyes so they'd reflect), his elegant attire, and his unmistakable Old World elegance combine to paint the portrait of an attractive, not repulsive, monster. The fact that Dracula seems to feed exclusively on pretty young women, preferring to make his male victims into ghoul-like slaves, addresses the underpinnings of eroticism associated with the act of vampiric blood-drinking. Christopher Lee went on to portray Dracula again in the 1958 film *Horror of Dracula*, where the erotic appeal of the vampire was more plainly addressed, with a tagline to the poster announcing Count Dracula as "the terrifying lover who died . . . Yet lived!" No other film had so explicitly presented the count as a potential object of desire before.

Francis Ford Coppola's 2000 remake of the film sets the events of the film again in the Victorian era, positioning the vampire as a figure of erotic sexuality at war with repressed Victorian mores. But Coppola's Dracula is more about romance than sex—this Dracula is motivated by longing. Adding a subplot missing from Stoker's novel, the filmmaker made Dracula a figure of intense romantic melancholy: Both his immortality and his vampirism seem to be caused by a broken heart after the death of his wife hundreds of years previous. (Vampirism and heartbreak have been connected before in fiction, but rarely quite so explicitly.) Dracula's need for blood is an explicit need for life and rebirth, for love and humanity (though the stolid legal clerk played by Keanu Reeves quickly twigs to the vampiric nature of the ladies inhabiting Dracula's castle with no more than their wanton sexuality to go on—vampires, in other words, are quickly identifiable by their unusually high level of physical attractiveness).

There is, of course, more to the world of screen vampires than the Count. Shortly after Coppola's *Dracula* came out, another vampire movie was released, one that ramped up the presentation of the vampire as romantic object and sex symbol: *Interview with the Vampire*, based on the Anne Rice book by the same name. The vampires of *Interview* are stylish bad boys who haunt the nights of antebellum New Orleans, feeding on the beautiful and lost. Oceans of lace spill from their wrists and they have attractive, pearly fangs. You get the sense they're more afraid of leaving the house without perfect hair than they are of sunlight or crosses. These vampires fear damnation, though—they're essentially lonely, cut off from humanity, and believe themselves to be cursed. They're able to fall in love and form romantic attachments, even with humans, though their love takes the form of turning those humans into fellow vampires—who are not always happy with the result. Whether they'd make good boyfriends is somewhat up for debate—they're certainly attractive, and seem like the sort of boyfriends who would bring flowers and recite poetry, but their love almost always ends in doom and a messy death.

So what do we learn from all this? Vampires are *depressed*. They're positively emo. Even though they have everlasting life and good looks, none of them ever seem very happy about it. At least until you get to *The Lost Boys*, which presents the vampire as party boy. The eponymous boys of the title are a group of California vampire teens whose motto is, "Sleep all day. Party all night. Never grow old. Never die. It's fun to be a vampire." And it *is* fun. This is the vampire as ultimate juvenile delinquent—they spend their time razzing cops, riding motorcycles on the beach, and jumping off bridges with their '80s rocker hair flying. Oh, and occasionally they eat somebody. If Edward had this much fun all the time, which I have to admit it doesn't sound like he does from what I've heard, I'd say Bella should stay with him. Especially if he also wears a feather earring like David, the leader of the Lost Boys. The Lost Boys are eventually dispatched by the Frog brothers, a duo of ordinary teenagers who've picked up their vampire-killing pointers through exhaustive comic book research (at one point they read a comic book called *Vampires Everywhere*, urging a cohort to consider it a "survival manual"). They use Super Soakers full of holy water to put the vampires down. The real downside here is that the one female member of the Lost Boys, Star, never seems to have any fun—she has to drink blood out of a bottle and doesn't get to ride a motorcycle on the beach. Instead she stays home, dusting the lair. I'd say that the members of the Lost Boys would make pretty good boyfriends except that they clearly don't know how to take a lady's needs into account. Girls want to have fun, too.

So what can we learn from all this tireless horror movie-watching? Well, Aunt Charlotte has a view, but she doesn't think you're going to like it. Then again, that's why she's the advice columnist and you're not. Both vampires and werewolves, it seems, are intensely romantic figures, though in different ways. The werewolf is tied to the cycles of life, the earth, and the moon. Werewolves are very much a part of nature, and as such are deeply in touch with their animal selves. They're fierce, feral—and dangerous. Vampires, on the other hand, being immortal, have wrenched themselves free of life's natural cycles and stand very much apart, inhabiting almost another plane of existence. They're distant, romantic, cold—and also dangerous.

The lesson to be learned from all this is that if Bella wants to stay safe, she should date neither a vampire nor a werewolf, but find herself a nice human boy. Preferably one who already knows about the supernatural. One great truth we absorb from movies is that geeky boys who read comic books have a lot of useful knowledge in the clutch—they know how to fend off not just vampires and werewolves, but presumably mummies, zombies, and even Frankenstein's monster. In the end, they're your best bet to stay alive and get to college. Whoever pays for it.

Lots of love,
Aunt Charlotte

* * * * *

Cassandra Clare was born in Tehran and spent much of her child-hood traveling the world with a suitcase full of books. She now lives in New York City, whose urban landscapes inspired her *New York Times* bestselling young adult fantasy novel *City of Bones*. You can also find her work in the upcoming young adult anthologies *Geek-tastic* and *Vacations from Hell*. She prefers vampires to werewolves.

A Moon ... A Girl ... Romance!

A Note from the Periphery

James A. Owen

Picture this book cover: A chesty, muscular, long-haired (but clean-shaven) he-man clutches an equally chesty, long-haired, exceptionally beautiful woman in a low-cut dress. Under a full moon, the maiden leans back seductively, offering her neck (and a whole lot more) to the ravenous he-man. Now substitute "vampire" for he-man; and make the woman a little less voluptuous, a bit plainer, and likely too clumsy to bend backward and still look sexy. What have you got? Twilight as "bodice-ripper." Think that's a stretch? Not really, says James A. Owen, who claims the Meyer books are not teen novels, fantasy fiction, or tales of horror, but rather good old-fashioned romances.

The best scientist is open to experience and begins with romance—
the idea that anything is possible.

—RAY BRADBURY

I'm going to open an essay critical of simplification with a simple statement: Stephenie Meyer's Twilight books are not teen books, or fantasy fiction. They're Romances. But before you build a complex argument to that simple statement, please bear with me and I'll clarify.

There is a nearly ubiquitous human tendency to reduce things to their simplest elements, and nowhere is this more evident than in discussing literary genre. It doesn't matter what the genre is; they all get a reductionist beating from the simplicity stick sooner or later. Thus, Science Fiction becomes rockets, and ray guns, and robots. Fantasy becomes unicorns, and elves, and faeries. Mystery becomes trench coats, and bullets, and dames. And then there's Romance. This genre, or at least the perception of it, has been simplified more than any other. It has been reduced well past the hallmark creations and the original, broad concepts to a single simple image: that of the ripped bodice.

Answers.com says a "bodice-ripper" is "a work of popular fiction characterized by scenes of unrestrained romantic passion." That pretty much sums it up. Books in this category have managed the near-impossible feat of being identifiable by the same iconic imagery almost regardless of differences in plot and story. There is a chesty, muscular, long-haired (but clean-shaven) he-man clutching an equally chesty, long-haired, exceptionally beautiful woman in a Scarlett O'Hara dress. There is usually a moon present, and the couple is more likely than not somewhere outside a palatial estate with floral gardens and a fountain. Windswept cliffs are optional. And the maiden is usually felled in a faint. (I could have said she was swooning, but "felled in a faint," being far more florid language, may actually better underscore the point I'm making, so there you go.) The term "bodice-ripper" itself implies that at some point in the story the, ah, "hero" forcefully impresses his will upon the protesting-but-not-really maiden, ripping her bodice (the close-fitting upper part of a woman's dress) in the process.

What is particularly unfair about this simplification is that Romance, as a genre, has a long and distinguished history, including what many consider the high watermark, Jane Austen's *Pride and Prejudice*. A lot of exceptional literary stories have been written within the Romance genre since then, and even more stories that were unremarkable by literary standards but perfectly serviceable if you consider that they Do the Job: tell a brief story with a clear plot and plenty of passionate action.

What *is* fair about the simplification is that it works. Everyone reading this essay pictured a variation on the imagery I described, and knew precisely what it meant. And considering the genre of Romance novels also represents more than half of the books sold in this country each year, it's interesting that among my friends and colleagues I was hard-pressed to find anyone who would admit to having read one. Those who were most adamant that they would never be caught dead with a bodice-ripper in their possession were also the most appalled at my suggestions that 1) they were, in fact, avid Romance readers, and 2) they each had at least one, and possibly three, Romance novels on their shelves (or on the nightstand, or in the bathroom, etc.) at that very moment.

I could make those statements in full confidence, because they (and almost everyone else I know) are readers of Stephenie Meyer's Twilight series. And the Twilight series is *all* about Romance, even if it's not a bodice-ripper.

Meyer's output (which consists of three novels as of this writing: *Twilight, New Moon,* and *Eclipse*) has been marketed as Young Adult, but all that means (speaking from personal experience) is that the editor who liked it the most happened to be a YA editor. J. K. Rowling has nearly obliterated the lines that once existed between YA publishing and mainstream adult publishing. Readers are looking for good fiction, for well-told stories—and the source is no longer as important as it once was. If *Romeo and Juliet* had been published today, the ages of the characters alone would have made it an automatic pass for an adult publishing line; once published, however, it would have found readers of all ages.

Meyer's characters, like Rowling's, are teens when the story begins, but get progressively older as the series continues, dealing with more and more adult scenarios all the time. So the YA title, while functionally descriptive of Meyer's stories (which certainly deal with the angst of moving through adolescence), is incomplete. There is something more to the work. And that's where the vampires and werewolves come in, because the Twilight series isn't *just* a Romance. It is, in fact, much, much more. It's also Fantasy, touched with a hint of the Supernatural, and books in those genres (unlike the common perception of predictable Romance) are about possibility.

Supernatural tales, especially where they deal with creatures like vampires, are easy to classify as Horror (which is yet another example of my genre simplification theory. Horror equals scary stuff, blood, and anything by Stephen King), but as with the other genres, much simplification can blind a reader to a wealth of story. Overlooking a book because of the surface trappings might be a practical way to pare down a reading list, but on occasion it means missing a real gem. It might mean missing something extraordinary, that is greater than the sum of its simplified genre parts.

Supernatural Romance is nothing new. In fact, one of the most successful authors of the last few decades, Diana Gabaldon, has founded a publishing empire on that blended genre with her popular Outlander series. Her heroine, Claire, a nurse from World War II–era England, finds herself magically transported to eighteenth-century Scotland, where she meets (and falls in love with) a young Scot named Jamie. And the rest is literary and publishing history.

What is significant about the supernatural/magical/time-traveling elements of the stories Gabaldon tells is that they are almost entirely inconsequential to the narrative. It's a device she uses to facilitate the meeting of the characters. And while their differing cultures and backgrounds give her a lot to play with plot-wise, Gabaldon never veers from the core concept that it's the romance that matters. It's the interplay between Jamie and Claire that we care about. How they came together (which would have been 90 percent of the focus of a Science Fiction or Fantasy novel) is less important than the fact that they did.

Whether by design or writerly instinct, this is the same objective Stephenie Meyer has pursued with her star-crossed lovers Edward and Bella. The romance between the two is handled as deftly as a sailboat in a stiff wind: it's the handling of the boat, and the tension the wind creates against the sails, that pulls you along and propels you forward. Only with Meyer's story the tension is created by the fact that Edward is a vampire, who is constantly worried about whether he can control his desires for Bella. A third player, Jacob, brings additional narrative tension (call it a crosswind) due to the fact that he is Bella's friend and Edward's adversary, thanks to the reality that his people—werewolves—are enemies of the vampires.

Again, this is not a new story she tells throughout the series, not based on the surface elements alone. Just in the last few years, the film *Underworld* and its sequel explored the whole vampire-versus-werewolf dichotomy, which has been a staple of supernatural fictions since the days of Bela Lugosi and Lon Chaney, Jr., in Hollywood. What makes it work for Meyer is that as with Gabaldon's books, the supernatural elements are only devices to bring the characters together. What happens after that point is where we, as readers, become engrossed in the story. And Edward and Bella's story is all about Romance.

The tensions between Edward and Bella that are caused by his peculiar state of being are essentially metaphors for adolescent angst, but the metaphors work because they are already familiar to readers. There is an attraction between Edward and Bella— she's the insecure newcomer, he's the dark, beautiful outsider. Bella sees him do all the sorts of things that an infatuated girl might imagine of the object of her affection: Edward performs feats of strength and speed; he is difficult to injure; and he seems able to read minds. What makes these things compelling is that he really can do all of that because he's a vampire. And he's attracted to Bella, because he is drawn to her blood.

Everything that follows is based on that attraction, because for Edward to give in to it would mean either death or conversion for Bella. And Edward refuses to take a life or to bite a human (much less initiate the changes that might make him or her into a vampire).

Vampire lore has always mingled elements of sensuality with implied (and outright) violence. The blood lust of a vampire can be a very sensual thing—to a point. And Meyer knows this. Edward is constantly examining his desires and his motives . . . but so is Bella. At one point later in the trilogy, she asks if he's more desirous of her body, or her blood.

To Edward, it's an expression of love to not give in to his desire to, well, taste her blood. The potential is always there because of *what* he is; but it's kept in check because of *who* he is.

When Bella is poisoned by a bite on the hand from another vampire (unfortunately named James), it falls to Edward to save Bella by sucking out the venom. And it's here that the Romance elements roar back in at full force.

Both Edward and James, as vampires, want to taste Bella's blood, but while Edward holds himself in check because of his feelings for her, James simply wants what he wants. This type of love triangle is a staple of the Romance genre. Both vampires have the same urges, the same drive for violence; Bella even knows, fully and consciously, that Edward has those feelings and must constantly suppress them in order for her to remain unharmed. Is there any better definition of Romantic Love?

Meyer takes it a step further by making the means of Bella's salvation what Edward both wants and fears: to taste her blood himself. This is what makes the triangle, and the resolution of that scene interesting. What makes it Romance is that Edward is able to overcome his own desires, and do only what is needed to save her.

The angle Meyer places on that choice is that Edward doesn't think he has a soul, believing he lost it in his darker years, when drinking blood and taking human lives were acceptable to him (even if under the justification that he would only kill evil humans, avoiding more worthy ones). Edward isn't worried so much for his own soul, but for Bella's, and even more so, for her very life.

An accident on her eighteenth birthday (involving a paper cut) puts Bella in danger from Edward's entire family, who had thrown her the party. The attention drawn to her from the association with the Cullens, Edward's family, brings more vampires to her world, as well as the werewolves, who have a shaky truce with the vampires. The truce holds only so long as no human is bitten—and Bella is determined not to grow so old that Edward might lose interest in her, imploring him to help her become a vampire herself. In the process, Bella's father has become more and more wary of Edward, at one point grounding Bella for an indefinite period of time. Edward leaves Bella, only to return—star-crossed lovers are often parted, but always find a way to come together again—even when Edward reluctantly acknowledges that it may be inevitable for them to be together, he makes one last request: for her to marry him before her metaphoric, and in some ways literal, death.

It will come as no surprise to anyone who sees the literary parallels that Bella's favorite story (which she has memorized) is *Romeo and Juliet*, or that at one point she is reading *Wuthering Heights*.

When the Romance genre was first defined, it arose from the broader concept of Romanticism itself. This was a movement of heroic and noble sagas, bursting with strong emotions and aesthetic experiences. It was about the exploration of possibilities. Even the earliest Science Fiction (which of all the modern genres is the one most open to possibility) was termed "Scientific Romance." It was only with the advent of the twentieth century and the more narrow definition of Romance novels as being about two people exploring a relationship, often in a very predictable fashion, that the term both gained acceptance and lost power. But the Sci-Fi/ Fantasy genre has retained the reputation it started with: a genre filled with wonder. And so the combination of those elements with Romance is exceedingly compelling, allowing Romance to, in effect, return to its true Romantic roots.

As a term of popular culture, Romance means "bodice-ripper." But I'd like to suggest that with her Twilight series, Stephenie Meyer has achieved a Romance in the old-fashioned sense as well: She's created a work that explores possibility through the relationship between a girl and a deathless boy. If you were to remove all the supernatural elements, the core story would remain: lovers who come from different backgrounds and cultures, whose families have values that clash. There is an unsteady courtship, and then a declaration of desire, and then tragedy and parting. There is a period of mourning and loss, then redemption and reconciliation. There is bonding, and rebuilding, and finally, the opportunity to choose to create a permanent union out of the love they share—a love that literally may never die.

The addition of the supernatural elements is what makes the story itself so easy to process and absorb. The supernatural is in part about the fear of the unknown, and a new love is as unknown as it gets. How much more potent it is to be told that along with the desire to share a life is the equally strong desire to take it—which is resisted because of the love one has for the other. And the symbolism in *Romeo and Juliet* cannot be overlooked here; Bella is willing to give up her life—in becoming a vampire—in order to share a life of a different kind with Edward.

What makes that Romantic is that while it seems that Bella would be giving up a great deal—namely, her humanity—to marry him, from another point of view she would be setting the stage for a great, immortal love story: By becoming a vampire, she would be negating the desire he has to taste her blood, which is the dark undercurrent that has affected their entire relationship. And if that were eliminated, all that would remain is his love for her, and hers for him. And it might be in that act that he would see that not only has Bella *not* lost her soul, but he never lost his own.

Depending on who you ask, *Twilight*, *New Moon*, and *Eclipse* could be whittled down to various simple, easily defined classifications. Teen coming-of-age novel? Easily so. There's enough adolescent angst to make older readers grateful they're reading the series as adults, and the high school hierarchies are dead-on enough to make teens wish they were aging faster. Supernatural/Horror? Well, that's a harder one to argue. It has werewolves and vampires, but—the anomaly of Steven King's classic *Carrie* aside—I'm unable to think of a horror book deserving of the name in which the denouement takes place at the prom. Romance? Most assuredly. Not so much in the "bodice-ripper" way, but rather in the original sense: the sense that anything is possible.

What's more extraordinary, though, is the idea that Meyer's books can be defined by the modern term as well, which says that there should be an "emotionally satisfying and optimistic ending." The paces Meyer puts her characters through are thrilling because they're recognizable: fears are fears, and anxieties, especially where love is involved, are pretty universal. But the books, the stories, the characters are also loved because, like a bodice-ripper, they are predictable. Like a modern Romance, we know that an optimistic ending is in the wings. And we are fully expecting an optimistic ending.

We always know Edward and Bella are meant to be together. We know, even when they are parted, that there will be a reunion. And we know, or rather we want to believe, that despite all the trials they endure, they will end up together, fulfilled, and happy. And that may be Stephenie Meyer's greatest achievement: that in a genre where anything can happen, she has presented a story where readers want to see happen exactly what we know is going to happen, and kept our attention every step of the way.

If you think I'm wrong, ask the average teen reader, the kind who dresses up for Edward and Bella's fictional prom, if they've ever willingly dressed up to act out a scene from *Romeo and Juliet*. The odds are good they'll say no—but mark my words: If Shakespeare had only made the Capulets vampires and the Montagues werewolves, it might have ended up an awful lot like the Twilight series, and freshman English would have been an awful lot more interesting.

• • • • •

James A. Owen has been working professionally as an illustrator and storyteller for more than two decades, which is notable mostly because he's still comfortably in his thirties. To date, in addition to numerous illustration and design projects, James has written and illustrated two dozen Starchild comics and books, a series of prose novels titled Mythworld, and *Here, There Be Dragons* and *The Search for the Red Dragon*, the first two books in the Chronicles of the Imaginarium Geographica, which is published by Simon & Schuster. James works at the Coppervale Studio, a 14,000-square-foot, century-old restored church in Northeastern Arizona. For more information, please go to http://www.coppervaleinternational.com.

Edward, Heathcliff, and Our Other Secret Boyfriends

Robin Brande

Stephenie Meyer, and through her, her Twilight heroine Bella, make no bones about loving the classic romances. The two are especially fond of Shakespeare's Romeo and Juliet, Emily Brontë's Wuthering Heights, and Jane Austen's Pride and Prejudice. But how do the classic heroes stack up against Meyer's contemporary (if classic in the truest sense) heroic vampire Edward Cullen? Romeo. Heathcliff. Darcy. Edward. Whose chivalry outshines the rest? Who overcomes the longest odds to win his lady's hand? Whose love promises more longevity than all the others'? Who wins the title "Classic Hero Idol"? Robin Brande casts her vote.

We all have our ideal, swoon-worthy romantic heroes: Aragorn in Lord of the Rings (sigh), Will Turner in Pirates of the Caribbean, Jack Shepherd on *Lost,* Justin Timberlake in "SexyBack"—

whatever. But in her Twilight series, Stephenie Meyer has handed us the dreamiest of lovers, so beyond our regular fantasies we're even willing to give up body heat in exchange for sleeping against the cold marble chest of that most perfect of formerly human men, Edward Cullen—giving hope at last to hundreds of men huddled in Antarctica with no sweeties to call their own. (Sorry, guys, but Edward means much more to us than chilly skin. Read on.)

In constructing her ideal mate, and giving him all the qualities a fifteen-year-old (okay, and older) girl needs in a romantic partner, Stephenie Meyer borrows some of the characteristics of other great lovers in literature. She drops hints throughout the series of who those men might be: Heathcliff from *Wuthering Heights*, Romeo from *Romeo and Juliet*, and Mr. Darcy in *Pride and Prejudice*. But can any of those guys possibly match up to the perfection that is Edward Cullen? Let's see.

Heathcliff, a.k.a. Scary Psycho Man

I'll admit that when I first read *Twilight*, I made the mistake of thinking it reminded me of Emily Brontë's *Wuthering Heights*—you know, the lovers who declare they can't live without each other, the smoldering but unconsummated passion, the windy moors (rainy Forks, whatever)—clearly Bella and Edward are Catherine and Heathcliff, right?

Ugh. So wrong. Have you read *Wuthering Heights* lately? I have. And Heathcliff is—let's be honest here—a total whack job. He's all about revenge and rage and torture. At one point he even strangles a little dog—can you ever imagine Edward Cullen doing that? Sure, he'd rip a grizzly or a mountain lion or a werewolf to shreds, but that's just good (vampire) business.

Yet despite all Heathcliff's obvious flaws, *Wuthering Heights* remains our heroine Bella Swan's favorite book—she rereads it often during the series.

Which drives Edward crazy. He can't understand Bella's fascination with Heathcliff and Cathy, nor can he see why those two have been ranked among the top romantic couples, along with titans like Romeo and Juliet and Elizabeth Bennet and Mr. Darcy. "It isn't a love story," Edward says of *Wuthering Heights*, "it's a hate story" (*Eclipse*).

Which is why Edward is my boyfriend. Because he's absolutely right: Heathcliff isn't a tragic, romantic figure, he's an obsessive psycho boyfriend from hell.

Just a few highlights from the Heathcliff file:

1. When Cathy marries Edgar "Girly-Boy" Linton instead of him, Heathcliff vows to take his revenge on Edgar and his family (because obviously Cathy had nothing to do with it. Ahem). Heathcliff sees his opportunity when he finds out Edgar's sister has a mad crush on him. He quickly seduces her, strangles her little dog just because that's how dating went back in those days (or maybe I misunderstood), and starts treating her like a servant the instant he marries her. Good times.

2. When the son of that union turns out to be even more sickly and whiny and incredibly annoying than even his Uncle Edgar, Heathcliff basically torments the boy into an early grave (although frankly, we can't blame him for that. Heathcliff's son could possibly be the most irritating character in all of literature).

3. Speaking of graves, when Cathy dies, Heathcliff tries to dig up her body so he can sleep next to it all night. And he tells himself that if he wakes up and finds her stiff and cold, he'll just pretend it's because the wind is particularly icy that night. Ewww. Let's leave the body where it is, shall we, lover boy?

What's disturbing is that, over time, both Bella and Edward begin to see the similarities between themselves and the *Wuthering Heights* lovers. Bella, like Cathy, feels torn between two men, and even though some of us would argue that Jacob Black in no way measures up to Edward Cullen (although, granted, Jacob does have a usefully high body temperature), Bella doesn't view the choice as either easy or obvious. She does, however, recognize that the two men in her life are a lot better than the ones in Catherine Linton's, since "neither one is evil, neither one is weak" (*Eclipse*). We can definitely give her that.

And even though Edward is scornful of most of Heathcliff's behavior, he does empathize with him over one thing: Heathcliff's decision not to force Cathy to choose between him and her husband, even if her husband is a weak, pasty-faced, whiny-boy of a man. Cathy's husband, on the other hand, does force a choice, and banishes Heathcliff from the house.

As Heathcliff explains it:

> And there you see the distinctions between our feelings: had he been in my place and I in his, though I hated him with a hatred that turned my life to gall, I never would have raised a hand against him. You may look incredulous, if you please! I never would have banished him from her society as long as she desired his. The moment her regard ceased, I would have torn his heart out, and drank his blood! But, till then—if you don't believe me, you don't know me—till then, I would have died by inches before I touched a single hair of his head!

(Notice the blood-drinking reference. Was Emily Brontë secretly writing the first girl-vampire romance? Why haven't any of those fancy British biographers caught on to that yet? Doesn't anyone read anymore?)

Like Heathcliff, Edward takes the high road and doesn't try to interfere with Bella's relationship with Jacob Black, even though

Edward—like the rest of us—can clearly see that Jacob is wrong, wrong, wrong for her.

But we won't quibble with all you Bella/Jacob shippers. Just know that you're sadly confused and need to reread the books.

Despite their few similarities, can we really say Edward and Heathcliff are anything alike? Let's review a few key points:

1. Edward is kind. He would rather hurt himself than see Bella hurt—for example, choosing in *New Moon* to leave her rather than continue exposing her to danger from his vampire family. Heathcliff, on the other hand, is happiest when everyone around him is suffering mightily. He'd like them all to die horrible deaths, and he does his best to assist them in that.

2. Edward is rational. Once he understands that Jacob Black is no threat to Bella, and in fact might offer her some protection when Edward is away, he cooperates by bringing Bella to Jacob whenever she wants—even though Edward knows Jacob is trying to steal Bella away from him. Heathcliff? Not so rational. See section about digging up dead body to sleep with it. 'Nuff said.

3. Edward is noble. He fights against his instincts, and drinks only animal blood (the vampire equivalent of being a vegan). He constantly risks his own life to save Bella and the people she loves. He resists taking her to bed, even though she's more than willing. Heathcliff exacts his revenge on everyone around him by cheating people out of their land, marrying a woman he despises, stealing children from their loving guardians just so he can torture them—the list goes on and on. Not a good date for Thanksgiving with your family.

Decision: Edward. By a WIDE margin.

Romeo, a.k.a. Mr. Puffy Shirt

So what about our man Romeo? Surely he would outdo Edward in the romance department, right? As Bella herself admits in *Eclipse*, she's always had a thing for Romeo—at least until she met Edward. So how did Edward take the lead?

This won't take long. Shakespeare may have understood love, but he really had no idea what would appeal to the young women of the twenty-first century. And to think people called him a visionary.

First let's see where Edward and Romeo are neck in neck:

1. Both Edward and Romeo know how to woo a woman. They declare their love honestly, specifically, and constantly—pretty hard to resist.
2. Both Edward and Romeo refuse to go for the fling, and instead insist on marrying the women they love.
3. Both Edward and Romeo vow that they can't live without the women they love, and then do their best to prove it when Bella and Juliet call their bluffs by appearing to kill themselves.

So it's pretty close, except for three critical differences:

1. Edward is there with Bella in person, and therefore much easier to snuggle up to than her former crush Romeo;
2. Edward is immortal, so it's a lot easier to establish a long-term relationship; and
3. Edward does not wear tights.

Decision: Edward.

Mr. Darcy, a.k.a. Mr. Perfect

But now let's look at Mr. Darcy. Because no one—NO ONE—can possibly compare to Darcy, even Edward Cullen—right? Mr. Darcy is dignified, noble, loyal, protective, romantic, powerful, heroic— everything any of us could want in a man. Plus he's terribly rich, which is definitely a turn-on.

But both Mr. Darcy and Edward have a lot to learn about manners. When the two of them first meet their future soul mates, both men are cold and offensive. In Darcy's case, here's the conversation our heroine Elizabeth Bennet overhears at the ball where they're first introduced:

> "Come, Darcy," said [his friend Bingley], "I must have you dance. I hate to see you standing about by yourself in this stupid manner. You had much better dance."
>
> "I certainly shall not. You know how I detest it. . . . Your sisters are engaged, and there is not another woman in the room whom it would not be a punishment to me to stand up with . . . You are dancing with the only handsome girl in the room," said Mr. Darcy, looking at the eldest Miss Bennet.
>
> "Oh! She is the most beautiful creature I ever beheld! But there is one of her sisters sitting down just behind you, who is very pretty, and I dare say very agreeable. Do let me ask my partner to introduce you."
>
> "Which do you mean?" and turning round he looked for a moment at Elizabeth, till catching her eye, he withdrew his own and coldly said, "She is tolerable, but not handsome enough to tempt me; and I am in no humor at present to give consequence to young ladies who are slighted by other men. . . ."

Okay, so that guy needs a good smack upside the head. But Edward doesn't come across as any friendlier when he first meets Bella in *Twilight*. They notice each other across the crowded lunchroom the first day she begins attending Forks High School. They're both intrigued—Bella because Edward is so unbelievably handsome, and Edward because Bella is the first human whose mind he can't read. So far so good.

But then right after lunch the two of them discover they're in the same biology class, where Bella is assigned to Edward's lab table. Here's how Bella sees it:

> Just as I passed, he suddenly went rigid in his seat. He stared at me again, meeting my eyes with the strangest expression on his face—it was hostile, furious. . . . I peeked up at him one more time, and regretted it. He was glaring down at me again, his black eyes full of revulsion. As I flinched away from him, shrinking against my chair, the phrase if looks could kill suddenly ran through my mind.

Yeep. Not exactly love at first sight.

But as we soon learn, there's a reason Edward reacts so strongly once he gets close to Bella: One whiff of her, and he feels an immediate and nearly uncontrollable blood lust toward her. It's all he can do not to lure her outside, jump her, and chug down all her blood. (Which can happen sometimes in a relationship—admit it.)

So here's where we first get a taste of Edward's nobility: First he tries to transfer to another class, and when that doesn't work he simply leaves town. Even when he returns to Forks, he stays as far away from Bella as he can, and treats her as coldly as possible so she'll want to keep her distance. But there's still that damn biology class—proving once again that biology is the deciding factor in any romance. You can't fight your hormones, or your vampire lust, or whatever your issue is. Some of us have dated guys simply because we liked the way their skin smelled. Even though they were sort of jerks otherwise. But back to Edward and Mr. Darcy.

Ultimately, despite their legitimate concerns over pursuing these women—in Edward's case, his fear that he'll kill Bella; in Darcy's, the disparity between his and Elizabeth's standing in society and the fact that her mother is an obnoxious pig—neither man can resist forever. The fact is that Bella and Elizabeth are just too remarkable to ignore.

Which leads to the most important parallel of all: As both Edward and Darcy succumb to our heroines' charms, we discover the hidden passion neither man seems to know he possesses. And best of all, once that passion is freed, it belongs to no one but our Bella and Elizabeth—which truly is every girl's fantasy. We all want to awaken the cold lover and find that he is hot *only for us*.

Darcy is awkward at expressing his feelings at first. He tells Elizabeth he loves her and wants to marry her, but he also lays out all the reasons why that's not such a great idea. Elizabeth, of course, turns him down, since no one wants to be told, in effect, "I love you even though I know it's a really stupid thing to do. But marry me anyway."

Edward does a far better job wooing Bella. Chapter thirteen of *Twilight* is one long courtship scene, beginning with Edward revealing what happens when his skin is exposed to direct sunlight (way more romantic than a guy showing you his scars). Then he confesses every thought, every feeling he has had about her from the moment they first met. What girl can resist that?

> "I wanted you to forget my behavior that first day, if possible, so I tried to talk with you like I would with any person. I was eager actually, hoping to decipher some of your thoughts. But you were too interesting, I found myself caught up in your expressions . . . and every now and then you would stir the air with your hand or your hair, and the scent would stun me again. . . ."

Hold up for a moment: "You were too interesting . . . I found myself caught up in your expressions. . . ." Sigh. What girl of any age wouldn't want to hear that from the guy she was obsessing over?

Who doesn't want to know she's been studied that closely—especially when all this time she thought the guy hated her?

Edward's confession to Bella that he wanted her to forget his behavior that first day is echoed at the end of *Pride and Prejudice* in Darcy's second attempt to ask Elizabeth to marry him. This time, Darcy has obviously learned some of the smoothness that comes so naturally to Edward:

> "My behavior to you at the time had merited the severest reproof. It was unpardonable. I cannot think of it without abhorrence. . . . The recollection of what I then said—of my conduct, my manners, my expressions during the whole of it—is now, and has been many months, inexpressibly painful to me. Your reproof, so well applied, I shall never forget: 'Had you behaved in a more gentlemanlike manner.' Those were your words. You know not, you can scarcely conceive, how they have tortured me. . . ."

Major points to both men for owning up to their errors. We like that in a fantasy boyfriend.

And finally, the last of their most important similarities: Both men make tremendous sacrifices to protect and save the women they love.

In Darcy's case, he tracks down Elizabeth's wayward sister and spends a lot of time, money, and effort to spare her from a life of ruin—in turn saving Elizabeth's and her family's reputation. And best of all, he does it without being asked and without telling Elizabeth he's going to do it—in fact, he swears her sister to secrecy. But the sister has a big mouth, and Elizabeth learns all. And good thing she does, since it's the final piece in Elizabeth's transformation. She is now officially in love.

In Edward's case, he makes an even greater sacrifice to keep Bella safe. He removes himself from her life when he realizes everymoment they're together puts her in grave danger:

> "I couldn't live with myself if I ever hurt you. You don't know how it's tortured me. . . . You are the most important thing to me now. The most important thing to me ever."

Stop right there, buddy. Sold. Make me your vampire queen.

But Edward isn't the only danger for Bella. He risks his life over and over throughout the series, battling good vampires and bad, in an effort to keep Bella safe. There's his brother, who wouldn't mind snacking on Bella at her birthday party; the coven of evil, non-vegan vampires who would like to hunt down Bella and tear her limb from limb; and the ruling class of vampires who don't really approve of humans hanging around too long without becoming either lunch or vampires themselves. Edward has to protect Bella from all of them, and even though he's immortal, he's not indestructible—killing him just takes a little extra effort.

So points to Edward for actually risking his life. Although Darcy would no doubt do the same, if only given the chance. (It's not his fault Jane Austen never thought of introducing vampires into her stories. Think of how beloved she'd be today if only she had.)

Ultimately, though, there's no question that Edward has to overcome far more than Darcy does to be with the woman he loves. Even though Darcy changes his whole personality from haughty to hot in his effort to win Elizabeth's love, the fact is Edward and Bella simply face greater obstacles—time after time after time. Their threats are of the life-and-death kind, and no matter how dreamy and noble Mr. Darcy is, he simply can't compete with the talents of an immortal vampire who is able to rip into ribbons anyone who threatens his mate.

Decision: Edward.

May the Best Former Human Win

There's no getting around it: Edward will always win against any of those classic romantic heroes, because he shares their best qualities while adding some that are all his own.

He is more selfless than any of them, making choices that he believes will benefit Bella no matter how much agony they cause him—think of his leaving her to spare her from any further danger, and later refusing to interfere with her relationship with Jacob.

He is more protective, perhaps because he is better equipped. Of course, the stakes are much higher when you're running with vampires and werewolves, but there's no question Edward has lifesaving skills none of the other men possess.

He is bare-hearted and honest, holding nothing back. Romeo had his pretty soliloquies, and Darcy can say a lot once he gets going, but no one gives you the blow-by-blow, this-is-why-I-love-you the way Edward does. In part it's because Bella seems to need that much convincing, but in part it's because it's obviously Edward's way of dealing with his emotions.

And finally, no one is as attentive to his lover's every mood, every gesture, every nuance as Edward is, and that's saying a lot. Heathcliff gives him a good run on obsessiveness, and both Darcy and Romeo notice the highlights of their girlfriends' features (hair, skin, eyes, etc.), but Edward spends both day and night studying Bella's face, listening to her talk in her sleep, watching for blushes and paleness and probably even one eyelash being out of place. With his highly attuned senses, he has her on hi-def all the time. And while that might make some women uncomfortable, there's also something very appealing about being that important—essentially being the center of the universe—to someone so extraordinary.

It's official: Edward Cullen wins—at least against this competition. Would he beat out Aragorn from Lord of the Rings? Well, now, that's a whole other discussion. . . .

• • • • •

Robin Brande is the author of *Evolution, Me, and Other Freaks of Nature*, and an avid fan of all things insanely romantic. Following completion of this essay, she immediately threw herself into a three-day binge of Darcy-infused chick flicks, including *Bridget Jones's Diary*, the BBC version of *Pride and Prejudice* (yes, the one with Darcy in the wet shirt), and the most recent Keira Knightley version of *Pride and Prejudice*, with a Darcy almost hot enough to make her forget her extreme crush on Colin Firth. Almost.

To Bite, or Not To Bite; That Is the Question

Janette Rallison

Conflict is at the heart of every work of fiction. On the surface, it might seem exterior conflict is at the heart of the Twilight series. After all, it's about vampires fighting vampires, and werewolves hunting vampires, and vampires stalking people and people getting torn to shreds. Right? Or do the stories go much deeper? Is exterior conflict the nucleus of the Twilight series? Janette Rallison argues that, in fact, interior conflict drives the series, and it all centers around free will. Do vampires have to give in to their blood lust? Must werewolves and vampires, bitter enemies, fight to the death? To bite or not to bite? To shred or not to shred? These questions and more fuel the inner conflicts central to Meyer's writing, as Rallison illustrates.

What's your definition of a bad day? A fight with a friend? A speeding ticket? How about being attacked by a vampire and painfully turned into the undead, then realizing you must wander for eternity fighting off a craving to kill people? Yeah, that would pretty much be a bad day.

Carlisle, the leader of the Cullen clan of vampires, had this bad day and (we can assume) many other bad days that followed. Stephenie Meyer doesn't skimp when dishing out problems for her characters. Seriously, if you were Cinderella and could choose someone to be your fairy godmother, you wouldn't want it to be Stephenie Meyer. Sure, she could come up with the ultimate prince charming to take you to the ball, but he might kill you afterward.

Anyway, this particular bad day of Carlisle's, when he was attacked and transformed into a vampire, started the ball rolling for the Twilight series, but also defined it. Because Carlisle doesn't follow suit with the rest of the vampires. He realizes he has a choice and doesn't give in to his bloodthirsty impulses.

Edward tells Bella,

> "When [Carlisle] knew what he had become . . . he rebelled against it. He tried to destroy himself. But that's not easily done. . . . He jumped from great heights. . . . . He tried to drown himself in the ocean . . . but he was young to the new life, and very strong. It is amazing that he was able to resist . . . feeding . . . while he was still so new. The instinct is more powerful then, it takes over everything. But he was so repelled by himself that he had the strength to try to kill himself with starvation. . . . So he grew very hungry, and eventually weak. He strayed as far as he could from the human populace, recognizing that his willpower was weakening, too. For months he wandered by night, seeking the loneliest places, loathing himself.
>
> One night, a herd of deer passed his hiding place. He was so wild with thirst that he attacked without a thought. His strength returned and he realized there was an alternative to being the vile monster he feared. Had he not eaten venison in his former life? Over the next months his new philoso-

phy was born. He could exist without being a demon. He found himself again."

At times over the years, Carlisle saved a few of his dying patients, transformed them into vampires, and taught them his peaceful ways. One might question the wisdom of that decision, as turning someone into a vampire is generally a bad thing for society, but we can forgive him easily enough for creating Edward. Besides, Carlisle's main goal in life is to save lives. This is shown in *New Moon* when Bella falls and slices her arm open. All the other vampires clear the room (or are dragged away), because the smell of her blood is too tempting. Even Edward, who loves her more than anything, doesn't breathe after her first drop of blood is shed: "'I can handle it,' he insisted. But his jaw was rigid; his eyes burned with the intensity of the thirst he fought."

Only Carlisle is able to remain calm with so much blood around. Years working as a doctor have made it so he barely notices the scent anymore, even though Bella is sure that, "Clearly, this was much more difficult than he made it seem." When Bella asks him what he enjoys about his work he answers, "What I enjoy the very most is when my . . . enhanced abilities let me save someone who would otherwise have been lost. It's pleasant knowing that, thanks to what I can do, some people's lives are better because I exist."

When Bella tells him that he is trying very hard to make up for something that was never his fault, that he didn't ask for this kind of life and yet has to work so diligently to be good, he answers with, "I don't know that I'm making up for anything. Like everything in life, I just had to decide what to do with what I was given."

All of that pain, all of those self-struggles—and when you come right down to it, Carlisle is just a minor character in the series. Meyer saves her biggest inner conflicts for her main players.

Let's consider Edward for a moment. Yes, I know that if you're reading this essay there's a good chance you've already considered

Edward quite a bit. If you're one of the millions of teenage girls who've read the series, you may have considered Edward while gripping the book to your heart and murmuring his name. But even romantic icons don't have it easy.

First off, Edward is a vampire. And although many guys would not see a downside to superhuman strength, incredible good looks, a large fortune, and immortality, Edward does. He is afraid he has no soul. Edward believes in God, Heaven, and Hell, but he doesn't believe there is an afterlife for vampires.

Still Edward is trying to make good with his life or at least keep from doing damage to humanity. He has sworn off killing people and taken up the "vegetarian" lifestyle Carlisle's family lives. Then comes a remarkably hard struggle. Bella moves into town and the smell of her blood is practically irresistible to him. He compares it to being a drug addict and tells her that it's as though Bella's blood is his brand of heroin.[1]

Talk about your poor first impressions. She walks into class, sits next to him, and he spends the remainder of the hour thinking of different ways to kill her. This is not the usual way romances start out. As he describes it, Bella was some kind of demon, summoned straight from his own personal hell to ruin him.

But even drug addicts are able to make a choice about their actions, and so is Edward. As he thinks of ways to lure her to her death, he fights each idea back, thinking of his family and what it would do to them. With a tremendous amount of willpower and a quick trip to Alaska—we can assume things didn't turn out well for a few polar bears along the way—Edward feels that he is able to face Bella again with strength and composure. Poor Edward. Meyer isn't going to let him get off as easily as that. He comes back home and immediately falls in love with her.

---

[1] This is sort of how I feel about chocolate, but I digress.

Now he is caught between a rock and a hard place (even for a marble-like vampire). He wants to be with Bella even though he craves her blood. He takes her out on a date. And what a first date it is. He tells her to make sure she informs someone that she is going off with him in order to give her extra insurance that he'll bring her back instead of, you know, eating her somewhere along the way.

Well, no one ever claimed that Edward doesn't know how to sweet-talk a girl. After a brief internal struggle in the meadow, Bella's fate is determinedly decided.

> "I couldn't live with myself if I ever hurt you. You don't know how it's tortured me." He looked down, ashamed again. "The thought of you, still, white, cold . . . to never see you blush scarlet again, to never see that flash of intuition in your eyes when you see through my pretenses . . . it would be unendurable." He lifted his glorious, agonized eyes to mine. "You are the most important thing to me now. The most important thing to me ever."

He comments that he would have fared better if he had killed her that first moment, and yes, he is probably right. Because it isn't just the constant lure of her heroin-like blood that will torment him now. His love for Bella will bring him to make even more painful choices.

The first choice comes at the beginning of *New Moon* when he is in so much control over his vampire impulses that even Bella's slashed arm doesn't deter him from protecting her. Now that the pesky *should-I-eat-you-instead* deterrent to love is out of the way, one would think things would be easier for the couple. But one would be wrong.

It is Edward's looking out for Bella's best interest that causes the next problem. He doesn't want to turn her into a vampire because he doesn't want her to lose her soul. That is more important to him than being with her in an immortal life on earth. At the same time, he realizes that hanging out with vampires, even his own family, is dangerous to a girl who, with one drop of spilled blood, could easily be turned into a Happy Meal.

In *Twilight* he tells her,

> "I should have left long ago. . . . I should leave now. But I don't know if I can."
>
> "I don't want you to leave," I mumbled pathetically staring down again.
>
> "Which is exactly why I should. But don't worry. I'm essentially a selfish creature. I crave your company too much to do what I should."

In *New Moon* he undoes that choice and tries to make a better choice—one that is undoubtedly harder than his constant struggle not to kill her. He chooses to leave her for her own good.[2] It is never his love for her that is the issue. When he thinks she is dead, just like Romeo he is ready to forfeit his own life as well. Even though his departure seemed like the cruelest thing he could do to Bella, he had been thinking of what was best for her all along.

This, one would think, would be the hardest choice Edward would ever have to make regarding Bella. I mean, sure he figures she'll move on and fall in love with another guy, but at least he doesn't have to stay there and watch it happen. Well, not until *Eclipse* anyway, when Meyer makes him do just that.

Bella, in Edward's absence, has been hanging out with a guy—and not just any guy. He is Jacob Black, who happens to be a werewolf and every vampire's sworn enemy. Not only has Bella been seeing him, but she insists on continuing to see him after Edward

---

[2] Very noble of him, even if it did make the middle of *New Moon* an empty void for die-hard Edward fans. Personally, by the time he came back I was quite fond of Jacob.

returns because Bella and Jacob are friends. Well, she's a friend and Jacob is in love with her. And well, when you come right down to it, Bella is in love with him, too, and realizes that she and Jacob are actually soul mates. See, some boyfriends might have a problem with that, especially when Bella gives Jacob a particularly romantic—okay, way more than "particularly," it was more like curl-your-toes romantic—kiss as he goes off to fight an army of vampires.

Readers who are cynical of men have been buying the superhero strength, the psychic abilities, and the way certain characters sparkle like crystal in the sun, but at this point they may pause for a moment and say, "Hey wait a minute—is this fiction?" Would a guy who is so madly in love with a girl that he wants to die without her—would he be okay with all of this? Wouldn't he be angry enough to, I don't know, yell, sneer, give her an ultimatum?

But Edward doesn't do any of these things, which is why approximately three bazillion readers are in love with him. (The rest are in love with Jacob—it was a *really* good kiss.) Edward is still choosing to go against natural impulses and is thinking of what is best for Bella. When he comes upon her after her goodbye kiss with Jacob, she is hoping an avalanche will put her out of her misery so she doesn't have to face him. But Edward's expression is soft and his eyes are full of understanding. He tells her she is only human. In fact, it's clear that Edward understands Bella's love for Jacob better than she does.

> "When I left you, Bella, I left you bleeding. Jacob was the one to stitch you back up again. That was bound to leave its mark—on both of you. I'm not sure those kinds of stitches dissolve on their own. I can't blame either of you for something I made necessary. I may gain forgiveness, but that doesn't let me escape the consequences."

He continues and tells her,

"I'm not going to make you choose between us. Just be happy and you can have whatever part of me you want, or none at all, if that's better. Don't let any debt you feel you owe me influence your decision."

If that speech isn't enough to make you love Edward, then you are even more heartless than the hordes of vampires who run around in this series. Really, undead or not I know women who would abandon everything for a guy that understanding.[3]

Now let's take a look at the series's second gasp-at-him-gorgeous guy, Jacob Black. (Let's take a really good look and wish the book came with full-color illustrations.) Jacob, because he had the misfortune to end up in a Stephenie Meyer novel, also has his share of problems. First of all, he and his friends are werewolves. This is something he didn't want or choose but had thrust upon him because vampires moved in next door. And okay, transforming into a giant wolf with superpowers does have its cool points, such as speed, strength, and being able to protect your community by munching vampires into tiny pieces. But there are some definite drawbacks. When Bella first catches up to Jacob after his change, he is bitter—no, furious—at what has happened to him. Even talking to her is hard. He must take deep, deliberate breaths, trying to calm himself. He is so mad his hands shake.

He tells her, "I'm not good enough to be your friend anymore, or anything else. I'm not what I was before. I'm not good." He also tells her, "If I get too mad . . . too upset . . . you might get hurt." In fact, one of the werewolf pack's girlfriend, Emily, has already been hurt and she bears the scars—giant disfiguring slashes across one side of her face—from when her boyfriend Sam got mad and lost control for just one moment.

---

[3] I bet Edward does laundry and dishes, too.

The wolf pack also has a psychic connection that works well when they are hunting, but which gets invasive at other times. They can have no secrets from one another. They hear every thought, no matter how private, hurtful, or embarrassing. Personally, most people I know would be upset if someone read their e-mail. Having every desire and memory broadcast to nine other people would be a less-than-welcome experience. And if all this isn't bad enough, when Sam, the lead wolf, gives an order, the others must obey. No matter how badly Jacob wants to explain his situation to Bella, he can't. Sam has forbidden it, and the words won't come out of Jacob's mouth.

But these are not the worst of Jacob's problems. His worst problem is that the girl he loves is in love with a vampire, his mortal enemy. Most people in Jacob's position—having Edward as a rival—would give up and move on to someone who's more attainable. A princess or duchess of some small country, perhaps. But Jacob fights for Bella's attention. He tries using logic. He points out an eagle in the act of plummeting down toward the ocean to catch a fish.

> "You see it everywhere. . . . Nature taking its course—hunter and prey, the endless cycle of life and death. . . . And yet, you don't see the fish trying to plant a kiss on the eagle. You never see *that*."

Jacob is also not above using manipulation to win Bella. He encourages her to sneak away from the Cullens and see him. He tells her that perhaps he will let the vampires finish him off—knowing that Bella will beg for him to come back, that Bella will kiss him. And yet as much as he wants Bella, as strong as his feelings are for her, he, too, has a choice about his actions. At the end of *Eclipse* he realizes that Bella is being torn apart because she loves both Jacob and Edward, so Jacob tells her, "I'm not going to cut you in half anymore, Bella." He gives up what he wants the most for what he thinks is best for Bella.

The conflict between Edward and Jacob is mirrored by their cultures. Vampires and werewolves are natural enemies. Like cats and dogs (supposing that cats and dogs were huge, fast, and had supernatural powers). Like Republicans and Democrats (assuming politicians were young and incredibly good-looking). Like my healthy New Year's resolutions and Snickers bars (you get the idea). The peaceful Cullens and equally peaceful Quileutes don't get along even with a truce and boundaries in place.

In the beginning of *Eclipse*, vampires and werewolves can't even put aside their differences to fight Victoria, a common enemy. She is able to escape because the werewolves and vampires turn on each other instead of pursuing her. When Jacob and two of his pack brothers come to Bella's graduation party, trouble starts almost immediately. Jacob doesn't want Bella to leave the room until she's explained what is wrong, and he puts his hand out to stop her and Alice from leaving. In an instant—literally, in this case, because vampires can move so fast—Jasper is standing on the other side of Jacob with a terrifying expression. (It's no wonder, really, that Bella doesn't like parties. She doesn't seem capable of going to one without the risk of bloodshed. Which, if nothing else, should make her wedding an interesting read.)

Alice tells Jacob that lots of vampires are coming their way. There will be a fight and it doesn't look good for the Cullens. It would perhaps be logical for the wolf pack to cheer at this point, or at least burn campfires in celebration the way they did when the Cullens picked up and left town at the beginning of *New Moon*. Or they could let the vampires fight it out and then pick off the survivors. It would be a tidy solution to that nasty vampire infestation they have in the neighborhood.

But there is one difference now. Both Jacob and the Cullens realize that Bella's life is at stake. For Bella, they are willing to form a new alliance, and for the rest of the book they work together as a team to protect her.

Last but not least in this procession of overcoming one's given nature, there is Bella, the main character. She has neither superpowers nor immortality. If one were to listen to her (and we won't because she has, like, every guy in all three books in love with her), she isn't even very pretty. She does have one overpowering characteristic though: her love for Edward. Before she's even gone on her first date with him she is irrevocably lost in the throes of adoration. He tells her to make sure she informs someone she is going off with him as added insurance that he'll bring her back, but she doesn't. She doesn't want to cause any problems for him should he succumb to his temptations. (One would hope that she at least wore some really repulsive-smelling perfume.)

When Edward leaves her in *New Moon* she never recovers. In fact she starts courting danger because she feels closer to him when she is at risk in some way. When Bella and Edward are finally reunited she retains no ill feelings about being so painfully dumped. Jacob asks her how she can forgive him for it, and she simply tells him that there is nothing to forgive. In *Eclipse*, Jacob compares her love for Edward to a drug and says, "I see that you can't live without him."

But even this all-consuming love doesn't stop Bella from making choices, doesn't stop her from walking away from Edward, his love, and his protection. In *Twilight*, when she thinks James is holding her mother captive, she willingly leaves Edward, hoping that her own life will buy her mother's safety. In *Eclipse* she is ready to stab herself in the hopes that her spilled blood will distract the vampires, thereby saving Seth's life. Bella is willing to give up what is most precious to her—her life with Edward—in order to save others.

For a series in which everyone seems to be handed some very powerful predispositions, it is always—from the beginning to the end—a story about choices. Even Alice, who can see the future, really can't. Because the future changes with each choice that is made. Unlike the Oracles who plague Oedipus and other unfortunate Greek characters, and unlike so many fatalistic nineteenth-century novels in which characters seem to be just dominos in life's unhappy game, no one's fate is set in stone in the Twilight series. The future is made and undone with every choice a character makes. At the end of *Eclipse*, when Bella asks Alice if she can still see her as a vampire, Alice explains, "I'm only as sure as you are, Bella. You know that. If you were to change your mind, what I see would change."

And readers are left to wonder if Bella might. After all, Meyer tells us in *Eclipse* that Bella has "Two futures, two soul mates. . . ." It's her choice, and no one is excused from the responsibility of choice because of his or her nature. Bella sums up this philosophy very succinctly to Jacob when she thinks that the werewolves are responsible for some missing hikers' deaths: "It's not what you are, stupid, it's what you do!"

And what these characters do time and time again is rise above their more selfish dispositions. Perhaps this is why we love them so much. If even vampires and werewolves can forge their own destiny—can become noble and admirable by the choices they make—then there is hope for all of us.

* * * * *

Janette Rallison is the author of eight popular young adult novels, including *All's Fair in Love, War, and High School*, *It's a Mall World After All*, and the upcoming *Just One Wish*.

Janette has five children who keep her well-supplied with plot ideas, sometimes even making cameo appearances in her novels. She likes to write romantic comedy because there is enough angst in real life, but there's a drastic shortage of both humor and romance.

She is eagerly awaiting the next Twilight novel (and betting on Edward).

The Great Debate

Rachel Caine

> There has been much debate about what, exactly, lures female readers to vampires in general and to Edward Cullen specifically. We all know Edward is hot (despite being cold as mortuary marble, and just as hard). But why do we think so? Is our unnatural attraction to biting and sucking Freudian in nature and, if so, is that appropriate for young adult readers? What if the discussion went on the air as an actual, televised debate? Rachel Caine takes us in front of the cameras and behind the scenes in her campy Great Debate.

DEBATE HOST: Welcome to the most popular reality show on high-numbered cable television: **The Great Debate!** We have two teams of very learned, articulate scholars with us to debate an exciting and timely topic: **Resolved: Vampire-themed fiction represents thinly veiled sexuality and violence. Therefore, vampire fiction is not suitable for young adults, and in particular Stephenie Meyer's** *Twilight*, **which has brought**

vampire-themed young adult fiction to the forefront, is not appropriate for young adult readers.

Boos and hisses from the audience.

DEBATE HOST: With us today, arguing that vampire fiction is unsuitable for young adults, are Professor Nelda Harlen-Price, head of the English Literature department at the Skokie Academy for the Arts, and Professor Hans Scheller of the University of Classical Education, author of the monograph *On The Sexual Content and Repressive Nature of Folklore-Based Fictional Adaptations.*

Reluctant applause from studio audience.

HARLEN-PRICE: Happy to be here.

SCHELLER: *Ja.*

DEBATE HOST: Advocating the right of young adults to read vampire fiction are two emerging experts in the field, Vampluvrgrl1111 of San Diego, California, whose recent blog, "If You Don't Love Vampires, You Suck, And So Not in a Good Way," was so popular that it crashed the entire West Coast server network for approximately sixteen minutes.

VAMPLUVRGRL1111: *And* I brought down LiveJournal because more than 20,000 people tried to friend me at the same time. Oh, you can call me Mel.

DEBATE HOST: We also welcome Psychosister23, another prominent vampire expert on the Internet. Do you have a real name you'd prefer we use during the debate?

PSYCHOSISTER23: That is my real name.

DEBATE HOST: [*clears throat*] Then let us commence. I call this debate to order. We previously flipped a coin to determine precedence, and by virtue of this, Professor Harlen-Price will first state the argument of the overall position.

MEL: Why can't we go first?

DEBATE HOST: I'm sorry, but we do follow standard Lincoln-Douglas debating rules here on our show and—

PSYCHOSISTER23: I don't know who Lincoln Douglas is, but I'll bet he's a hater. Don't make me flame you. I've brought down fandoms, man. All I have to do is put a bulletin on MySpace, and you are *gone*.

MEL: They're going to bore people into changing channels before you even get to us.

DEBATE HOST: We'll hold our total initial arguments to no more than two minutes. Is that acceptable?

Whispered conversation between Mel and Psychosister23.

PSYCHOSISTER23: Whatever.

HARLEN-PRICE: It's clear to everyone that vampire-themed literature contains adult concepts, in particular sexual content, as well as a significant propensity for gruesome violence.
    The vampire is one of the most enduring and resilient archetypes of modern literature, and this archetype reached its zenith

with the introduction of the character of Dracula in Bram Stoker's 1897 novel. Although based on folkloric concepts that attempted to find supernatural explanations for the entirely natural processes of decomposition after death as well as various illnesses, the vampire as a romantic figure clearly did not emerge until—

MEL: We're not here to debate moldy old Dracula. And you're already at a minute.

HARLEN-PRICE: *As I was saying*, the vampire as a romantic figure clearly did not emerge until after the publication of *Dracula*. Although not a success initially, this novel became ingrained in public consciousness over time and, with the appearance of various film adaptations from *Nosferatu* to, of course, *Dracula*, the concept of vampire as a type of protagonist, if not romantic hero, became part of popular culture.

   However, it's important to examine the psychological and cultural underpinnings that led to this particular phenomenon. The vampire mythos was perfectly suited as a subconscious analog for the oppressive Victorian attitudes toward sexuality, especially the dangers of a woman's sexuality being released. Where in older eras vampires simply killed their victims, from the time of *Dracula* onward the act of biting and sucking has been turned into a sexual release, and in fact vampires frequently indulge in actual sexual activity in addition to the psychosexual biting. Clearly, none of this is at all suitable for young readers, who are at a very critical stage of their own normal sexual development. I have no objection to vampire literature aimed at an adult audience, but young adults are simply not capable of self-analysis, and thus cannot react in an age-appropriate way to the overwhelming stimuli—

MEL: TIME'S UP, BITCH. Also, you *suck*.

DEBATE HOST: Ah . . . unfortunately, Professor, we'll have to come back to you for the remainder of your initial statement. I'm sure you'll get to the subject of our debate in due course. Mel, I believe that you have the honor of making the initial argument for your position.

MEL: Damn straight. First of all, let's get right to the subject of this debate. *Twilight* is a completely awesome book. Bella: awesome. All her friends: awesome. The town: awesome.

PSYCHOSISTER23: Get to the point.

MEL: I *am*, keep your thong on already. [*deep breath*] *Twilight* is an awesome book because Edward Cullen is made of awesome, with awesome sauce and awesome sprinkle topping, and that's all there is to it.

Portions of the audience erupt into wild cheers; other portions seem deeply confused. Mel and Psychosister23 high-five.

MEL: Article one: Edward is hot.

PSYCHOSISTER23: You can stop there if you want. We win!

MEL: Article two: Edward is old, but he doesn't look like my grandfather. Which is so cool, that he can be old *and* beautiful.

PSYCHOSISTER23: Also, hot.

MEL: What she said. Article three: Edward tries to avoid Bella, and she thinks he hates her, but we all know deep down that it's just because he's truly madly deeply in love. Which is *so* awesome, because we know they're going to come together somehow.

PSYCHOSISTER23: I wanted him for myself.

MEL: Well, yeah, but let's face it, he was Bella's from the beginning. So, article four: Edward ends up saving her life, which was the last thing he wanted to do, because he is just that good. He can't help being a hero.

PSYCHOSISTER23: Doesn't count as much as his awesome hotness, though.

MEL: Hey, *my* statement. Go blog if you don't like it.

PSYCHOSISTER23: You suck.

MEL: You're right, Edward is hot, though.

PSYCHOSISTER23: Yeah, that's true. Okay. Peace.

MEL: Article five: Edward trusts Bella enough to tell her the truth about himself and his family, even though *she* doesn't see herself as worthy of him or his trust—she thinks she's clumsy and awkward and ugly. And he's strong enough not to bite her when she wants to be bitten, which—let's face it—is hot.

PSYCHOSISTER23: Dude, get to the incredible hotness of the kissing!

MEL: I *would* if you'd stop interrupting me!

PSYCHOSISTER23: Article six: Edward is an awesome kisser. Vampires are usually all about the fangs and sucking, but no, Edward is *romantic*. And that's so hot.

DEBATE HOST: Mel, Psychosister23, I'm afraid your time has run out. To sum up—the "Against" side of the debate has established its position that vampire fiction represents suppressed sexual urges, and Stephenie Meyer's *Twilight* contains elements that are inappropriate for the young adult audience they target.

HARLEN-PRICE: Just so.

DEBATE HOST: And the "For" side of the debate . . . has . . . established . . . that even if their opponents' point is true, it doesn't matter because Edward Cullen is hot?

Girly squeals from audience.

MEL: We are *so* winning.

DEBATE HOST: Professor Scheller, you may now pose your initial challenge to the other team's position.

SCHELLER: Young woman, how is Edward Cullen's physical attractiveness an indication of the literary merit of the work in question?

MEL: Duh, Professor. If you want to get teen girls to read about vampires, you don't want to give them some overdressed opera-cape guy in a dusty castle in Europe, and the idiot who wants to stake him, and the nitwit girl who can't make up her own mind and if she does decide she likes the chocolate instead of the vanilla, she is automatically tramptastic.

PSYCHOSISTER23: Because that is bull[*bleep*] to us.

SCHELLER: But you must acknowledge that much of what you find attractive about the character of Edward comes from classical sources of the *other*: the outcast, the god-king in disguise—

MEL: Don't got to acknowledge nothing, but we like the bad boy aspect, too. Look, the important thing is *Twilight* made those stories real to *us*. Bella mopes around about her life, sure, but she *does* stuff. And she falls in love. And she writes love notes and has daydreams and knows that true love is the only real magic in the world.

SCHELLER: So your argument is that unless the vampire appears in the guise of the familiar, he is less effective?

MEL: Dude, Stoker was writing about *modern life*. He wasn't writing some historical novel—he was like John Grisham or something, writing about things *his* readers thought were familiar and comfortable. And then he made them *unfamiliar* and *uncomfortable*. Your point was Dracula was sex, right? And sex was something to be afraid of, especially when it got the women all loosened up because you never knew what that might do to the whole family—

HARLEN-PRICE: That's an oversimplification of—

PSYCHOSISTER23: Welcome to the Internets, bitch.

MEL: The point is, right or wrong, he wrote about things that gave people shivers then, including *teh sex*. Stephenie Meyer is writing about things that give *us* shivers right now. She's giving us the familiar and making it glamorous and exciting and dangerous. She's opening up the boring and showing us the awesome on the other side.

PSYCHOSISTER23: Also, Edward is hot. Hotness never hurts.

Girly squeals from audience.

DEBATE HOST: All right. Psychosister23, you can now pose a question to the other team.

PSYCHOSISTER23: So, why can't girls under eighteen like vampires? What's so bad about it?

SCHELLER: Young lady, clearly you do not understand the Freudian symbolism that the vampire represents, which relates to the oral stage of psychosexual development—a perversion or dysfunction of this important stage of human development.

PSYCHOSISTER23: BITE ME.

SCHELLER: Exactly so. Also, the retreat of a vampire from the life-giving warmth of the sun can be seen as an infantile desire to retreat back to the womb, which vampire mythos symbolically links to the grave.

MEL: They can't just be night people? Look, if you read old school vampire stuff, you see that vamps used to be *badass*, man. They didn't just suck blood, they *ate people*. And forget about that daylight stuff, and crosses. That all came about later, as people got civilized and the dark side had to fear *something*.

HARLEN-PRICE: Well—actually—that's true.

MEL: [*nods regally*] Google, dude. It's a blogger's best friend. Anyway, my point is, as people got *less* afraid of the dark, vampires became *more* like us. Just kind of pale versions of people, with an addiction.

PSYCHOSISTER23: Meth heads on crack.

MEL: But they blend in. We're making them *us*. The thing about *Twilight* is that the Cullens are trying to blend in, trying to be human, and mostly they succeed . . . but it's when they don't fit in that we connect with them.

PSYCHOSISTER23: Put it this way: the Cullens can't totally blend in, no matter how hard they try, and *we* feel like that. Every one of us feels like that at some point, but some of us go to school every day feeling like we'll never be part of the human race.

SCHELLER: Vampire as metaphor for the outcast. *Ja.* I said that!

MEL: Suck-up.

PSYCHOSISTER23: So wait, why was vampire stuff bad for us? I fell asleep.

HARLEN-PRICE: It's inappropriate. Young people do not have the proper frame of reference to understand the massive buried sexual power represented by the figure of the vampire, and the symbolism of the stake, the fangs—

MEL: Wait, is this *Jeopardy*? What is . . . Penetration. SCORE!

DEBATE HOST: Please allow the professors to continue.

Mel mutters. Psychosister23 glares.

HARLEN-PRICE: In vampire literature, creating a new vampire clearly serves as a metaphor for sexual contact, particularly when you examine the fact that it is an *exchange* of bodily fluids, not merely the act of feeding, that creates the new vampire—implying that the victim must become a partner in his or her own destruction. This is utterly unsuitable for young readers, young female readers in particular, who are in many ways already disposed to believe in romantic notions of death and a lack of consequences to sexual activity.

MEL: Clearly, you haven't been reading YA literature lately, or you'd know that it's really all about the danger and the consequences. Anyway, you just made the case for parents *wanting* us to read about vamps. Cautionary tales and such.

Psychosister23 offers a high-five.

MEL: Save it, I'm not done yet. Let's go back to our Edward Cullen Hotness Theory. Edward is hot not just because he's hot . . . well, hot, and old, and an outcast (but in a cool way) . . . he's hot because he doesn't want to bite Bella.

PSYCHOSISTER23: Oh, he wants to bite her.

MEL: But doesn't.

PSYCHOSISTER23: Hot.

SCHELLER: So you are saying that this act of restraint is an important lesson for young adults?

PSYCHOSISTER23: Look, we live in a world where we can get anything we want right now, where our parents live their lives on credit.

Instant gratification. We don't have relationships, we have hookups. We don't know how to wait. We also don't know good things until they're gone. Because Edward *won't* bite her, Bella learns about his world, and about what love really is. If he bit her, it'd probably have been *wham, bam, fang you ma'am.*

HARLEN-PRICE: And yet because of his reluctance to engage in psychosexual activity with Bella, Edward brings her into his world, which is extremely dangerous, and in fact has grave consequences for Bella herself.

MEL: So are you saying you *wanted* her to get bitten? I thought your whole point was just say no to the biting!

PSYCHOSISTER23: Well, she does pick up a fierce stalker. That's less than hot.

MEL: Not Edward's fault.

SCHELLER: Ah! Yet Edward is, in fact, the root cause of this act of destruction! In this case, the vampire represents the feared adult world tearing away the vestiges of innocence, and, despite his best intentions, Edward therefore becomes—even if by proxy— the vampire deflowering the virgin, which is a common theme in vampire literature—

MEL: Ewww. Man, you need therapy. If you want to play it like that, the bad guy vampire coming after Bella *was* the world, okay? But it was the big, bad outside world ripping apart their little circle of happiness, showing Bella that even the biggest, strongest boyfriend can't keep you safe all the time. That sometimes bad things happen to good people. And that's something young readers need to understand, too.

PSYCHOSISTER23: Man, that was scary.

MEL: True dat. I was shaking.

PSYCHOSISTER23: That was the *best* hurt/comfort.

HARLEN-PRICE: That brings up another of my objections. This type of fiction glorifies the experience of danger and pain in order to effect a dramatic point, which tempts young people to believe that they must experience the extremes in order to—

MEL AND PSYCHOSISTER23: BITE ME!

MEL: Look, bitch, drama is all about the extremes. Sure, you can make a drama about getting a C on a homework assignment, but who wants to read about that? We *live* that.

PSYCHOSISTER23: Some of us more than others.

MEL: Stories are supposed to be bigger. You know what I learned from *Twilight*? First, don't hate yourself—Bella thinks she looks like a dweeb, and that she's clumsy and uncoordinated. All she sees are her own shortcomings. But Edward sees her completely differently. Second, when you fall in love, let it happen, don't rush it along just because you can. Third, when a stranger calls and tells you they're holding your mom hostage in a dance studio. . . .

PSYCHOSISTER23: Totally call the cops.

MEL: Yeah, that would be better. But Bella was taking care of her mom even before the book started, so of course she wanted to take care of her when things got scary. And Bella *stepped up*. She was brave. She was strong. We need that kind of example in our lives, and it's more powerful when it comes from someone we relate to instead of from an adult *telling* us how to act.

DEBATE HOST: I believe we need to move on to final arguments. Psychosister23, please state the summary for your side.

PSYCHOSISTER23: Edward is hot. Bella is strong. We want them together *forever*. Also, Stephenie Meyer should come write at my house so I can read it over her shoulder. I'd be her best beta reader *ever*.

DEBATE HOST: . . . That's it?

PSYCHOSISTER23: Oh, all right. Look, the first mention of something like vampires is *6,000 years old*. Those were women who became vamps after losing a baby in childbirth. Then, when people needed to explain death from diseases they'd never seen before—bingo, vampires changed. Then Victorians took vampires into drawing rooms and made them the embodiment of all those dark, hidden sexy impulses they don't like to admit. Vampire stories are all about figuring out how to cope.

For us teens today, our stress comes from different stuff. We've got to contend with all kinds of evil, from pedophiles to bullies to teachers who don't care, absent parents, parents so crazed about your grades from the time you're born that you crack under the pressure—you name it, we can look around us and see it, or at least read about it on the Internet. Vampires—and in particular, the kind of vamps that Stephenie's writing about—represent three things to us: sex . . .

MEL: Because hey, hot!

PSYCHOSISTER23: Social power . . .

MEL: The Cullens *rule* even if nobody understands why they do. And even if they don't *want* to rule.

PSYCHOSISTER23: And personal immortality. Adults say, *Who wants to live forever?* Well, teens are the first ones to hold up their hands. Vampire stories are a way for us to explore what becoming an adult means, with all the scariness and darkness and responsibility. It lets us imagine and experience different times, different lives. It makes the past real to us in ways our history teachers *wish* they could, and it makes the future real, too, because even though we may want to give up sometimes, we never want those *characters* to give up—and that means we go with them. We see the future, we see something waiting for us even when we don't feel it inside sometimes.

MEL: BOO-yah!

PSYCHOSISTER23: *Twilight* isn't just about vampires and adventure and all that stuff, it's about Bella: an outcast misfit finding her place in the world and finding her strength. That's something we all need.

DEBATE HOST: Thank you. And now to—

PSYCHOSISTER23: EDWARD CULLEN IS HOT!

Wild cheers from the studio audience.

PSYCHOSISTER23: Okay, I'm done now.

DEBATE HOST: And now, the rebuttal from Professor Scheller.

SCHELLER: I . . . ah . . . well. . . . Vampires. . . . They are bad, and . . .
Oh, *Scheisse*, I admit it, I like the book.

HARLEN-PRICE: Professor!

SCHELLER: I have read it several times. Also, my daughter loves it.
And my wife as well.

HARLEN-PRICE: But—

SCHELLER: Vampires change through the ages, there is no denying
this fact. Certainly vampires were once monsters, and those
monsters took on aspects of the human psyche that we wished
to deny or repress. But what do they represent *now*, in this book?
I believe they represent precisely what Miss Psychosister23 has
said: sexual fulfillment, the lure of social power, and the
romance of adulthood and immortality, as well as the hidden
power of the outcast—Bella sees herself as a loner, a misfit, and
yet her very self-sufficiency is the core of strength that saves her,
and others. A very powerful combination indeed, and something
that all of us long for, perhaps most of all as lonely, awkward
teenagers.

HARLEN-PRICE: But we're arguing that it's *not* appropriate!

SCHELLER: I have switched sides. Keep up.

HARLEN-PRICE: Wait, is he allowed to do that?

DEBATE HOST: I don't know, but I really don't care. I think the book is
awesome.

Wild cheering from the crowd.

DEBATE HOST: Also, I can't wait to read the next one. Anybody else?

HARLEN-PRICE: Wait! I—repressed sexuality! Oral fixation! Penetration! Allegories of—you Internet people, with your Google and your pop psychology and your *hot guys*, whatever happened to real scholarly intercourse—

MEL: She said intercourse.

HARLEN-PRICE: DISCOURSE! I meant discourse.

MEL: Sure you did. Freudian much?

DEBATE HOST: I'm turning off your mic. These comments are entirely inappropriate for young audiences.

MEL: Troll.

PSYCHOSISTER23: Hater.

SCHELLER: I'm so ashamed.

DEBATE HOST: Okay, that's all we have for today. Please join us next week for more lively scholarly intercourse—

HARLEN-PRICE: DISCOURSE, BITCH!

MEL: That's the spirit!

DEBATE HOST: —about the pop culture topics that bring life to our lives. Until then, remember—

MEL: VAMPIRES RULE!

PSYCHOSISTER23: EDWARD CULLEN IS HOT!

SCHELLER: MY COLLEAGUE IS FULL OF SCHEISSE!

HARLEN-PRICE: I hate all of you.

DEBATE HOST: —Stephenie Meyer's *Twilight* is available at fine book-stores near you. Thank you, and good night.

● ● ● ● ●

Rachel Caine (a.k.a. Roxanne Longstreet Conrad, of many previous pop culture anthologies for BenBella's Smart Pop series) writes the young adult vampire series Morganville Vampires for NAL/JAM, as well as tons of other stuff. She is a big fan of Stephenie Meyer.

Also, Edward Cullen is hot.

Through the Wardrobe
Your Favorite Authors on C.S. Lewis's Chronicles of Narnia

Edited by **Herbie Brennan**, *New York Times* bestselling author of the Faerie Wars series

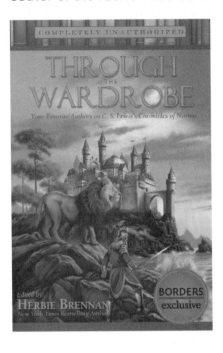

- Why is Prince Caspian the ultimate teenager?

- What do Hitler and the White Witch have in common?

- How come C. S. Lewis has such a big problem with lipstick, anyway?

Step through the wardrobe and into the imaginations of these sixteen friends of Aslan as they explore Narnia, from *The Lion, the Witch and the Wardrobe* to *The Last Battle*, from the heart of Caspian's kingdom to the Eastern Seas.

Exclusively in Borders stores April 2008

 @

Demigods and Monsters
Your Favorite Authors on Rick Riordan's Percy Jackson and the Olympians Series

Edited by Percy Jackson author **Rick Riordan**

- Which god would you want as a parent?

- Why is Mr. D the best camp director Camp Half-Blood could have?

- Would you want to be one of Artemis's Hunters?

- Why do so many monsters go into retail—and why are they never selling anything a demigod really wants?

Find out what your favorite authors think about Percy, Annabeth, Grover, Mr. D, Poseidon, and the rest of the gods, demigods, and monsters in the Percy Jackson and the Olympians series.

Exclusively in Borders stores May 2008

@

Secrets of the Dragon Riders
Your Favorite Authors on
Christopher Paolini's Inheritance Cycle

Edited by **James A. Owen**, author of *Here, There Be Dragons*

- How is raising a dragon like writing a book?

- What would Carl Jung think of *Eragon*?

- Why might Roran be the real hero of the Inheritance Cycle?

Ride along with your favorite authors as they dive deeper into Christopher Paolini's epic Inheritance Cycle, and the mysteries of the Dragon Riders.

Exclusively in Borders stores July 2008

 @